The Criticism
of
Cornelian Tragedy

The Criticism of

Cornelian Tragedy

A STUDY OF CRITICAL WRITING FROM THE SEVENTEENTH TO THE TWENTIETH CENTURY

by

Herbert Fogel

Long Island University

An Exposition–University Book

EXPOSITION PRESS   NEW YORK

EXPOSITION PRESS INC.

386 Park Avenue South   New York, N. Y. 10016

FIRST EDITION

EP 45726

To

MY MOTHER

Acknowledgments

I WISH to extend my sincerest appreciation to Professor Maurice Baudin for suggesting the subject and for his constant interest and advice during the writing of this volume. I wish also to take this opportunity to express my thanks for the research grant from Long Island University which helped to make possible the completion of this work.

H.F.

Contents

Introduction

THE manuals of French literature often present trends and authors in a compact, systematized fashion. Thus Pierre Corneille's tragedies are usually interpreted as conflicts between duty and passion in which duty is always victorious. Corneille is characteristically typified as the poet of will and his drama as an example of man's ability to use his will power and determination to conquer his feelings. Although some modern critics, in particular Brasillach, concede the conflict between duty and passion and the glorification of will, they maintain that other elements of Corneille's theater are just as important: an appraisal that suggested the need for a study of the various interpretations of Cornelian tragedy from the seventeenth century to the present.

The aim of this book is to trace the development of the legend that depicts Cornelian tragedy as the conflict between duty and passion and the subjugation of passions to nobler sentiments. The scope of the subject requires that the study be limited to major French critics whose works have survived. And because many critics may use the same general terms in their definitions of Cornelian tragedy while their interpretations of individual plays often reflect different attitudes, I will undertake a detailed study of four plays: *le Cid*, *Horace*, *Cinna*, and *Polyeucte*. The study, it is emphasized, will be limited to interpretations of the various periods that offer either marked contrasts or a complete adherence to tradition.

The study is divided into four parts. Seventeenth- and eighteenth-century evaluations of Cornelian tragedy are discussed in Chapter One, primarily because the precepts that regulated dramatic theory in the eighteenth century were essentially the same as those that governed the art of tragedy in the seventeenth. In the seventeenth century Cornelian tragedy was judged against the background of the classical doctrine that was being formulated at the time Corneille was writing his most celebrated plays. The rules of the doctrine that attempted to regulate the technique of theater were governed by one supreme criterion: verisimilitude. The seventeenth-century concept of verisimilitude was, in turn, closely related to the century's ideal of *bon goût* and *bienséance*. Such critics as Scudéry, Chapelain, l'Abbé d'Aubignac, Balzac, Boileau, Saint-Evremond, Mme de Sévigné, and La Bruyère judged Cornelian tragedy primarily against the seventeenth-century concept of verisimilitude and *bienséance*. Chapter One will attempt to determine whether or not these critics considered the glorification of will and the conflict between duty and passion to be the fundamental features of Cornelian tragedy.

While eighteenth-century dramatists generally followed the precepts of seventeenth-century doctrine regarding the technique of theater, their ideas of *bon goût* and *bienséance* were not the same as those of the earlier period. As a consequence, although Voltaire and La Harpe generally reinforced seventeenth-century judgments of Corneille's plays as to the technique of theater, their analyses of individual plays frequently showed marked contrasts to earlier interpretations.

Chapter Two is devoted to an analysis of evaluations of Cornelian tragedy during the first half of the nineteenth century. This era witnessed the birth of a new dramatic form, *le drame romantique*, which in essence was opposed to the classical concept of tragedy. While the most fervent advocates of the romantic drama (Hugo, Lamartine, Stendhal) clearly indicated their hostility to classical tragedy and to the Cornelian theater, these were defended by Janin, Nisard, and Saint-Marc Girardin. Because the critics discussed Cornelian tragedy primarily as it demonstrated, or not, the relative superiority of classical or romantic drama, it is only by studying their analyses of individual plays that one can see how their interpretations relate to those of the seventeenth and eighteenth centuries. The definition of Cornelian tragedy as conflict between duty and passion and the portrayal of man's limitless determination originated in the first half of the nineteenth century.

Chapter Three discusses Cornelian criticism in the second half of the nineteenth century. Brunetière, Lemaître, Faguet, Rigal, and Lanson, writing after the decline of romantic drama, did not in general judge Cornelian tragedy against the background of the classical or romantic theories of drama. Although their methods were not the same, it may be said that they sought to identify the principal elements of Corneille's theater independent of external circumstances. One of their main objects was the modification of earlier interpretations of Cornelian tragedy as a representation of the conflict between duty and passion. On the other hand, although they reinforced their predecessors' contention that a principal feature of Cornelian tragedy was the glorification of will, they were not in complete agreement as to their analyses of this theme. As a matter of fact, Faguet's interpretation of this aspect of Corneille's theater will be shown to have established a link between seventeenth-century and late-nineteenth-century ideas.

The reactions of twentieth-century critics, such as Dorchain, Rivaille, Schlumberger, Brasillach, Bénichou, Péguy, Adam, Nadal, Herland, Mornet, and Giroudoux, to Cornelian tragedy and to the interpretations of late-nineteenth-century critics are discussed in Chapter Four. As might be expected, twentieth-century critics generally attempt to modify the interpretations of their immediate predecessors: they seem to be emphasizing various significant features of Cornelian tragedy that earlier critics had only mentioned briefly. Chapter Four, then, will examine the effect of twentieth-century ideas on the earlier concept of a conflict between duty and passion and the glorification of will as the outstanding features of Cornelian tragedy.

The Criticism
of
Cornelian Tragedy

CHAPTER ONE

Corneille in the Seventeenth and Eighteenth Centuries

THE set of rules that modern literary critics call the doctrine of French classical tragedy was formulated in the first half of the seventeenth century. The Abbé d'Aubignac's *La Pratique du Théâtre*, published in 1657, presents the general attitude of the first half of the century towards dramatic art. It was used as a guide by most literary critics in the latter half of the century. It is significant, however, that Corneille's most celebrated tragedies were all written before 1657, and that although his plays were often severely criticized, sometimes even condemned, by his contemporaries, they nonetheless influenced the critics who were formulating the classical doctrine. On the other hand, Cornelian tragedy was in turn often to be judged against the background of the new doctrine.

The first major critical works devoted to Corneille were written during the quarrel of *le Cid*. The quarrel began with Corneille's publication, after the first criticism of *le Cid*, of his *Excuse à Ariste*, in which he boasted of owing nothing to others and claimed to be second to no French dramatist:

> Je ne dois qu'à moy seul toute ma Renommée.
> Et pense toute fois n'avoir point de rival.
> A qui je fasse tort en le traitant d'égal.[1]

The *Excuse à Ariste* was immediately answered by Mairet,

---

[1] A. Gasté, *La Querelle du Cid* (Paris: H. Welter, 1898), p. 64.

who declared that, after the judgment of the critics, posterity would understand that the success of *le Cid* was due entirely to Corneille's servile imitation of his predecessors.[2] Mairet was then joined by Scudéry, who published his *Observations sur le Cid*. Scudéry concluded that the subject was worthless, that the play violated dramatic rules, was poorly constructed, had many bad verses, and owed almost all its beauty to the Spanish dramatist.[3] After Mairet's and Scudéry's criticisms, numerous pamphlets were written both for and against *le Cid*. Most of the pamphlets were invectives, some rather insulting, either against Corneille or against Mairet and Scudéry.[4] Although the authors of most of these works preferred to attack the persons and family backgrounds of Corneille and his enemies rather than to offer concrete criticisms of *le Cid*, they characteristically judged the theater of Corneille primarily as it demonstrated, or not, their personal interpretations of the absolutes of classical theory. As a consequence, it is only by studying the formation of contemporary notions of the classical doctrine that one may understand the various reactions of the seventeenth century to *le Cid* and to Cornelian tragedy generally.

The three most important elements of the doctrine were that a play should be both useful and pleasing; that it should be likely or believable; that it should be moral and have a moral aim. The century was almost unanimous in agreeing that the dramatic poem should convey a lesson. Scudéry was one of the first to express this idea:

---

[2] *Ibid.,* p. 67, as cited from Mairet, *L'Autheur du Vray Cid Espagnol à son Traducteur François.*

[3] *Ibid.,* p. 80.

[4] Cf. *Lettre du Sieur Claveret au Sieur Corneille* and *Epistre Familière du Sieur Mayret au Sieur Corneille,* as cited in Gasté, *op. cit.,* pp. 251, 275.

Il faut savoir que le Poème du Théâtre fut inventé pour in-struire en divertissant.[5]

This opinion was sustained by Boileau in his *Art Poétique*, in which he said that a poet should join the useful to the pleasing and that—

> Un lecteur sage fuit un vain amusement,
> Et veut mettre à profit son divertissement.[6]

At the end of the century La Bruyère re-emphasized the moralizing function of all literature:

> On ne doit parler, on ne doit écrire que pour l'instruction; et s'il arrive que l'on plaise, il ne faut pas néanmoins s'en repentir, si cela sert à insinuer et à faire recevoir les vérités qui doivent in-struire.[7]

Corneille, however, rejected this didactic point of view and maintained that the purpose of art is to please and that the rules of dramatic poetry are only

> ... des adresses pour en faciliter les moyens au poète, et non pas des raisons qui puissent persuader aux spectateurs qu'une chose soit agréable quand elle leur déplaît.[8]

Although Corneille felt that the first purpose of dramatic poetry is to please, he was not entirely against application of the utilitarian principle:

> Pour moi, j'estime extrêment ceux qui mêlent l'utile au délect-

---

[5] Georges de Scudéry, *Observations sur le Cid,* cited in Gasté, *op. cit.,* p. 79.

[6] Nicolas Boileau-Despéraux, *Oeuvres* (Paris: Garnier, 1952), p. 184.

[7] Jean de La Bruyère, *Les Caractères* (Paris: Garnier, 1954), p. 63.

[8] Pierre Corneille, *Oeuvres* (2 vols., Paris: La Pléiade, 1950), Preface to *Médée,* I, 609.

able, et d'autant plus qu'ils n'y sont pas obligés par les règles de
la poésie; . . . mais je dénie qu'ils faillent contre ces règles,
lorsqu'ils ne l'y mêlent pas, et les blâme seulement de ne s'être
pas proposé un objet assez digne d'eux. . . . Pourvu qu'ils ont
trouvé le moyen de plaire, ils sont quittes envers leur art; et s'ils
pèchent, ce n'est pas contre lui, c'est contre les bonnes moeurs et
contre leur auditoire.[9]

The question of morality, the observance of the social
code, and the three unities, all have one important function
in dramatic art: their purpose is to render a play plausible.
Verisimilitude becomes, therefore, a principal aim of the
classical doctrine. In the seventeenth century a literary work
was apt to be judged immoral if it violated the rules of
bon goût and *bienséance*. Corneille's plays were often criticized on the ground that they were immoral, according to
the conventions, and therefore incredible. Scudéry, for example, violently criticized *le Cid* because he found
Chimène's willingness to marry her father's murderer both
improbable and shocking:

. . . on voit une fille desnaturée ne parler que de ses follies,
lors qu'elle ne doit parler que de son malheur, pleindre la perte de
son amant, lors qu'elle ne doit songer qu'à celle de son père;
aimer encore ce qu'elle doit abhorrer; souffrir en mesme temps,
et en mesme maison, ce meurtrier et ce pauvre corps; et pour
achever son impiété, joindre sa main à celle qui dégoute encor du
sang de son père.[10]

He indicated that while *le Cid* portrayed the conflict between duty and love, Chimène's willingness to marry Rodrigue illustrated the triumph of love over duty.[11] He also
charged that Chimène's words to Rodrigue, "sors vainqueur

[9] *Ibid.,* Preface to La Suite du Menteur, I, 1203.
[10] Gasté, *op. cit.,* p. 79.
[11] Cf. *ibid.,* pp. 90-91.

d'un combat dont Chimène est le prix" were words "dignes d'une prostituée."[12] He called Chimène weak because her love for Rodrigue prevented her from carrying out her obligation to avenge her father's death. In the eyes of most critics of the time of Scudéry, *le Cid* illustrated the triumph of love over duty and for this reason was considered suspect in terms of formal ethics.

Scudéry sought support for his criticism of *le Cid* by asking the Académie Française to analyze the play and his own judgments. The *Sentiments de l'Académie Française sur la Tragi-comédie du Cid* was primarily the work of Chapelain, who was in accord with current opinion on the utilitarian purpose of literature:

> Les mauvais exemples sont contagieux mesme sur les théâtres; . . . il y a grand peril à divertir le Peuple par des plaisirs qui peuvent produire un jour des douleurs publiques. Il nous faut bien garder d'accoustumer ny ses yeux ny ses oreilles à des actions qu'il doit ignorer, et de luy apprendre tantost la cruauté, et tantost la perfidie, si nous ne luy en apprenons en mesme temps la punition.[13]

While Chapelain refuted many of Scudéry's criticisms, he, like Scudéry, judged the play from the point of view of *bienséance* and verisimilitude; as a result he supported Scudéry's objection that *le Cid* violated accepted social ethics:

> . . . ny la bien-séance des moeurs d'une Fille introduite comme vertueuse n'y est gardée par le Poete, lors qu'elle se resout à espouser celuy qui a tué son Pere, ny la Fortune par un accident impreveu, et qui naisse de l'enchaisnement des choses vray-semblables, n'en fait point le demeslement.[14]

---

[12] *Ibid.,* p. 86.
[13] *Ibid.,* p. 360.
[14] *Ibid.,* p. 365.

This attitude of Chapelain's was expressed throughout the *Sentiments de l'Académie*.[15] Not only did Chapelain contend that *le Cid* violated the social code, but, like Scudéry, he particularly condemned the play because it illustrated the triumph of love over duty:

> Nous n'entendons pas neantmoins condamner Chimene, de ce qu'elle ayme le meurtrier de son Pere, puis que son engagement avec Rodrigue avoit precedé la mort du Comte, et qu'il n'est pas en la puissance d'une personne de cesser d'aymer quand il luy plaist. *Nous la blasmons seulement de ce que son amour l'emporte sur son devoir*, et qu'en mesme temps qu'elle poursuit Rodrigue elle fait des voeux en sa faveur. . . . Chimene luy donne presque à entendre qu'elle ne le poursuit que pour en estre plus estimée, et en fin souhaite que les Juges ne luy accordent pas la vengeance qu'elle leur demande.[16]

Although Chapelain did not condemn *le Cid* in entirety, he nonetheless supported most of Scudéry's major criticisms and concluded—in a less severe manner, to be sure—that the subject of *le Cid* was not good, that it was full of useless episodes, had many bad verses, was poorly constructed and offended *le bon goût* and *la bienséance*.[17] In spite of his criticisms Chapelain recognized that because of the naïveté and vehemence of Rodrigue's and Chimène's passions, the forceful and yet subtle manner in which they expressed their feelings, *le Cid* acquired

> . . . un rang considerable entre les Poemes François de ce genre qui ont le plus donné de satisfaction.[18]

The century was almost unanimously in agreement with Chapelain that even though *le Cid* violated the rules of

---

[15] Cf. *ibid.*, pp. 372-375.

[16] *Ibid.*, p. 275 (italics supplied).

[17] Cf. *ibid.*, p. 415.

[18] *Ibid.*, p. 374.

dramatic art, particularly those relating to verisimilitude and *bon goût,* there was in the play an inexplicable something that did not fail to charm the spectator. Sorel pointed out that Rodrigue's and Chimène's conflict between duty and love

> . . . donne tant de pitié et de plaisir ensemble, que jusques icy rien ne s'estoit veu qui eust tant attaché l'attention.[19]

This same attitude was reflected in Balzac's *Lettre à M. de Scudéri,* which stated that even if Scudéry's criticisms were irrefutable, Corneille would be able to console himself that

> . . . c'est quelque chose de plus d'avoir satisfait tout un Royaume, que d'avoir fait une pièce regulière.[20]

Boileau, who was generally hostile to Corneille, also admired *le Cid* and defended its inclusion of the love element:

> Je ne suis pas pourtant de ces tristes esprits
> Qui, banissant l'amour de tous chastes écrits,
> D'un si riche ornement veulent priver la scène,
> Traitent d'empoisonneurs et Rodrigue et Chimène.
> L'amour le moins honnête, exprimé chastement,
> N'excite point en nous de honteux mouvement.[21]

This observation, which recognized the impact of the play on its audiences, reflected an important opinion of the century and was reinforced by La Bruyère towards the century's close:

> *Le Cid* n'a eu qu'une voix pour lui à sa naissance, qui a été celle de l'admiration; il s'est vu plus fort que l'autorité et la politique, qui ont tenté vainement de le détruire; il a réuni en sa faveur des

---

[19] *Ibid., Le Jugement* du Cid, p. 231.
[20] *Ibid.,* p. 453.
[21] *Op. cit.,* p. 185.

esprits toujours partagés d'opinions et de sentiments, les grands
et le peuple. . . .[22]

Scudéry seems to have been the only major critic of the period who did not admit that while *le Cid* failed to observe
the essential precepts of the classical doctrine, it nonetheless
conveyed an impressive sense of beauty.[23]

The rules of morality and *bienséance,* as has been said,
were governed by the one supreme criterion of verisimilitude. The seventeenth-century verisimilitude should not be
confused with present-day realism. In the seventeenth century, verisimilitude, with its subtle overtones of *bon goût*
and *bienséance*, was the ideal form that reality assumed in
the opinion of the multitude. It was an ideal regulated by
universal and constant laws—a sort of superior reality. It
was in the name of verisimilitude that all the literary
battles started; it was the basis of all attacks on Cornelian
tragedy. This doctrine was presented in its most complete
and precise form by the Abbé d'Aubignac:

> . . . le vrai n'est pas le sujet de théâtre, parce qu'il y a bien des
> choses véritables qui n'y doivent pas être vues . . . Le possible
> n'en sera pas aussi le sujet, car il y a bien des choses qui se
> peuvent faire . . . qui pourtant seraient ridicules et peu croyables,
> si elles étaient représentées . . . Il n'y a donc que le vraisemblable
> qui puisse raisonnablement fonder, soutenir et terminer un poème
> dramatique: ce n'est pas que les choses véritables et possibles

---

[22] *Op. cit.,* p. 63.

[23] "Il est de certaines Pieces, comme de certains animaux qui sont
en la Nature, qui de loin semblent des Etoiles, et qui de près ne sont
que des vermisseaux . . . Mais que cette vapeur grossière[le jugement
du public] qui se forme dans le parterre ait pu s'eslever jusqu'aux
Galleries, et qu'un fantosme ait abusé le sçavoir comme l'ignorance,
et la Cour aussi bien que le Bourgeois, j'avoue que ce prodige m'es-
tonne, et que ce n'est qu'en ce bizarre evenement que je trouve le Cid
merveilleux." (Gasté, *op. cit.,* p. 71.)

soient bannies du théâtre, mais elles n'y sont reçues qu'autant qu'elles ont de la vraisemblance.[24]

D'Aubignac's interpretation of the principle of verisimilitude, about which the critics of the period were in almost complete agreement, was later supported by Boileau:

> Jamais au spectateur n'offrez rien d'incroyable :
> Le vrai peut quelquefois n'être pas vraisemblable.
> Une merveille absurde est pour moi sans appas :
> L'esprit n'est point ému de ce qu'il ne croit pas.[25]

It was for such reasons, and as a result of such attitudes, that the rules of *bienséance* and *bon goût* were related to the desire to achieve verisimilitude.[26]

Because Chapelain's criticism of *Le Cid* was founded primarily upon the fact that the play defied the rules of *bienséance* and therefore was not plausible,[27] he would have preferred, he said, that the ending of *le Cid* had revealed that the Count was really alive or that he was not Chimène's father. Chapelain's observation is an illustration of how the desire for verisimilitude, as a literary abstraction and carried to an extreme, can result in rendering a play more artificial than realistic. It would have been better, Chapelain said, if Rodrigue had allowed his love to win

---

[24] *La Pratique du Théâtre,* cited by R. Bray, *La Formation de la Doctrine Classique* en France (Paris: Nizet, 1951), p. 200.

[25] *Op. cit.,* p. 171.

[26] For example, the Abbé d'Aubignac, as cited from R. Bray, *op. cit.,* p. 49: "Il y a bien des choses qui se peuvent faire justement et sans honte, et que l'on ne peut expliquer ni même toucher sans blesser la bienséance."

[27] "Il y a des vérités monstrueues, ou qu'il faut supprimer pour le bien de la société . . . Le Poete . . . doit travailler plustost sur un sujet feint et raisonnable, que sur un véritable qui ne fust pas conforme à la raison." (*Sentiments de l'Académie Française,* cited in Gasté, *op. cit.,* p. 366.)

over his honor because "Rodrigue estoit un homme, et son sexe qui est comme en possession de fermer les yeux à toutes considerations pour se satisfaire en matière d'amour, eust rendu son action moins estrange et moins insupportable."[28]

Corneille presented his interpretation of the principle of verisimilitude in the prefaces to his plays and in his *Trois Discours*. In his Preface to *Médée*, before the quarrel of *le Cid*, he contended that the portrait painter and the dramatist have one important thing in common: the artist often paints beautiful portraits of ugly women while the dramatist may present beautiful imitations of an action that one should not imitate. He argued that the dramatist is not concerned with the morality of the character he depicts, but only with whether the actions he attributes to that character are supported by history or common opinion.[29] Thus his own interpretation of verisimilitude seemed to rest upon support in fact rather than to be the product of a literary abstraction.

An important precept of the classical doctrine, which ensues from the desire to create a semblance of plausibility and to adhere to the concept of *bienséance*, was that virtue should be rewarded and crime punished. It was, at least in part, as a result of this attitude that the Académie Française accused Chimène of being derelict in her duties. Corneille was never able to accept this idea, which he labeled, not a precept of art, but rather a custom borrowed

---

[28] *Ibid.*, p. 374.

[29] "Dans la portraiture, il n'est pas question si un visage est beau, mais s'il ressemble; et dans la poésie, il ne faut pas considérer si les moeurs sont vertueuses, mais si elles sont pareilles à celles de la personne qu'elle introduit. ... Je n'examine point si elles [les moeurs] sont vraisemblables ou non: ... il me suffit qu'elles sont autorisées ou par la vérité de l'histoire, ou par l'opinion commune...." (*Op. cit.*, I, 609.)

from the ancients. He declared that although the custom was prevalent during the time of Aristotle, it evidently did not please the philosopher, who said that it

> ... *n'a eu vogue que par l'imbécilité des spectateurs, et que ceux qui le pratiquent s'accommodent au goût du peuple, et écrivent selon les souhaits de leur auditoire.* ...[30]

Corneille then advanced the idea that—

> Le succès heureux de la vertu, en dépit des traverses et des périls, nous excite à l'embrasser; et le succès funeste du crime ou de l'injustice est capable de nous en augmenter l'horreur naturelle, par l'appréhension d'un pareil malheur.[31]

This notion concerning the concept of punishing crime and rewarding virtue was reaffirmed in his *Discours du Poème Dramatique*:

> Cléopâtre, dans *Rodogune*, est très méchante; il n'y a point de parricide qui lui fasse horreur, pourvu qu'il la puisse conserver sur un trône qu'elle préfère à toutes choses, tant son attachement à la domination est violent; mais tous ses crimes sont accompagnés d'une grandeur d'âme qui a quelque chose de si haut, qu'en même temps qu'on déteste ses actions, on admire la source dont elles partent.[32]

In his Preface to *Médée*, Corneille indicated his opposition to the generally accepted interpretation of verisimilitude; and throughout his career he never ceased to defend himself against the charge that many of his plays were not plausible. In his *Discours de la Tragédie* he advanced the idea that there are three types of tragic action: one follows history; another adds to history: the third type falsifies history. The first type is true, the second is sometimes plausible,

---

[30] *Ibid.,* I, 65.
[31] *Ibid.*
[32] *Ibid.,* p. 67.

and the third may be used only when absolutely necessary.[33] He emphasized that when the action is historically true it need not be plausible, and for support he referred to Aristotle, whose works were a guide to those who criticized Corneille.[34] He conceded that if an action is not founded upon historical evidence, it is then necessary that it be plausible.[35] The plausibility of *Héraclius* was suspect to critics who thought it highly improbable that a mother would expose her son to death in order to save the son of another person. Corneille countered that the action was historically true and therefore

> . . . il ne faut plus s'informer si elle est vraisemblable, étant certain que toutes les vérités sont recevables dans la poésie, quoiqu'elle ne soit pas obligée de les suivre.[36]

His opinion that what is historically authentic need not be plausible was also reflected in his *Discours du Poème Dramatique*:

> Il n'est pas vraisemblable que Médée tue ses enfants, que Clytemmestre assassine son mari, qu'Oreste poignarde sa mère; mais l'histoire le dit, et la représentation de ces grands crimes ne trouve point d'incrédules.[37]

As noted, Corneille's most important plays were written while the classical doctrine was being formulated by the critics; and in 1657 D'Aubignac presented the doctrine in

---

[33] Cf. *ibid.*, I, 111.

[34] *"Tout ce qui s'est fait manifestement s'est pu faire, dit Aristote, parce que, s'il ne s'était pu faire, il ne se serait pas fait."* (*Ibid.*)

[35] *"Nous avons une pente naturelle, ajoute Aristote, à croire que ce qui ne s'est point fait n'a pu encore se faire; et c'est pourquoi ce que nous inventons a besoin de la vraisemblance la plus exacte qu'il est possible pour le rendre croyable."* (*Ibid.*)

[36] *Ibid.*, Preface to *Héraclius*, II, 159.

[37] *Ibid.*, I, 60.

its most complete theoretical form. Corneille was almost alone in his opposition to what came to be the most generally acceptable interpretations of the doctrine, and although his plays increasingly indicated an effort to follow the rules, he manifested a marked distaste for them in his discussions on dramatic theory. Not only did Corneille's ideas concerning verisimilitude, *bienséance*, and the utilitarian aim of poetry differ from those of his contemporaries, but he attacked the very usefulness of rules that were based on formulations made centuries before his time.[38] He declared that he could enlarge or change these rules without scruple according to the needs of his subject, especially when they seemed to him to be absolutely incompatible with the events he wished to portray.[39] Knowing the rules and understanding how to adapt them to the theater of the period are two completely different things, and

> . . . pour faire maintenant réussir une pièce, ce n'est pas assez d'avoir étudié dans les livres d'Aristote et d'Horace.[40]

Corneille's argument against the absolute validity of Aristotelian maxims as interpreted by his contemporaries was based on the principle that science and art had progressed since the time of the ancients:

> Puisque les sciences et les arts ne sont jamais à leur période, il m'est permis de croire que les anciens n'ont pas tout su, et que de leurs instructions on peut tirer des lumières qu'ils n'ont pas eues.[41]

---

[38] "Comme les anciens avaient plus d'étude et de spéculation que d'expérience du théâtre, leur lecture nous peut rendre plus doctes, mais non pas nous donner beaucoup de lumières fort sûres pour y réussir." (*Ibid., Discours du Poème Dramatique*, I, 62.)

[39] Cf. *ibid.,* Dedication of *La Suivante,* I, 466.

[40] *Ibid.*

[41] *Ibid.,* Preface to *Clitandre,* p. 223.

Towards the end of his career Corneille considered Aristotle's and Horace's rules more of a hindrance than an aid to progress:

> Leurs règles sont bonnes; mais leur méthode n'est pas de notre siècle; et qui s'attacherait à ne marcher que sur leurs pas, ferait sans doute peu de progrès, et divertirait mal son auditoire. On court, à la vérité, quelque risque de s'égarer, et même on s'égare assez souvent, quand on s'écarte du chemin battu; mais on ne s'égare pas toutes les fois qu'on s'écarte. . . .[42]

Corneille was not without support in his opposition to the doctrine of Aristotle and Horace. Saint-Evremond, for example, censured the observance of the precepts for the same reasons:

> Si Homère vivait présentement, il ferait des poèmes admirables, accommodés au siècle où il écrirait. Nos poètes en font de mauvais, ajustés à ceux des anciens et conduits par des règles, qui sont tombées avec des choses que le temps a fait tomber.[43]

Like Corneille, Saint-Evremond held that no rules are perfect enough to govern all people at all times.[44] Corneille's remonstrances against servile acquiescence to the classical doctrine reveal an insight that placed him ahead of his time; in fact, it was just such ideas that later would touch off the famous quarrel of the ancients and the moderns.

In the second half of the century Cornelian tragedy was judged not only against classical doctrine, but also against Racinian tragedy. With the advent of Racinian tragedy the ideal of dramatic art became simplicity and clarity. It was especially concerned with the human heart.

---

[42] *Ibid.*, Preface to *Agésilas*, II, 905.

[43] Charles de Saint-Evremond, *Oeuvres,* ed. A. Gidel (Paris: Garnier, 1866), p. 166.

[44] "Il faut convenir que la *Poètique* d'Aristote est un excellent ouvrage; cependant il n'y a rien d'assez parfait pour régler toutes les nations et tous les siècles . . . Corneille a trouvé des beautés pour le théâtre qui ne lui étaient pas connues." (*Ibid.*, p. 106.)

For these reasons seventeenth-century tragedy more and more eliminated external events, and what remained, the workings of the human heart, developed into the psychological tragedy, or tragedy of character. Cornelian tragedy, on the other hand, was essentially a tragedy of intrigue. Corneille's preference for extraordinary and complicated subjects, evident throughout his theater, is especially noticeable in his later plays. As a matter of fact, he gave his own definition of the unity of action in his *Discours des Trois Unités*: the unity of a tragedy is contained in the successive perils that confront the principal character. A tragedy may contain several perils or actions without disrupting the unity of the play so long as each peril evolves logically from the preceding one and continues to endanger the life or well-being of the principal character.[45] Another criticism often leveled against Corneille was that his plays were too complicated. An illustration is D'Aubignac's critique of *Sophonisbe*, the substance of which was applicable to all of Corneille's plays.[46]

Still another criticism involved Corneille's whole treatment of love, which he always claimed held second place in his plays.[47] Corneille would prefer to be admonished for

---

[45] Cf., *op. cit.,* I, 118.

[46] ". . . le plus grand défaut d'un poème dramatique . . . est lorsqu'il a trop de sujet et qu'il est chargé d'un trop grand nombre de personnages différemment engagés dans les affaires de la scène, et de plusieurs intrigues qui ne sont pas nécessairement attachées les unes aux autres. . . ." (Cited in R. Bray, *La Tragédie Cornélienne devant la Critique classique—d'après la querelle de Sophonisbe* 1663 (Paris: Hachette, 1927, p. 17.)

[47] ". . . j'ai cru jusques ici, que l'amour était une passion trop chargée de faiblesse, pour être la dominante dans une pièce héroïque: j'aime qu'elle serve d'ornement, et non pas de corps." (Cited in Saint-Evremond, *op. cit., Lettre de M. de Corneille à M. de Saint-Evremond pour le remercier des louanges qu'il lui avait données dans la dissertation sur "l'Alexandre" de Racine,* p. 151.)

having created his women too heroic than to be praised for having feminized his heroes.[48] Here too his treatment of love was contrary to the attitude of the time, for as the century developed, the study of sentiment was the principal occupation of the *honnête homme* and the most popular topic of the salons. Thus it was not only the conflict with poetic doctrine that caused his difficulty, but the fact that his concern for the grandiose was not in accord with a general attitude that with the passage of time had become more effete.

The opinions of the century on the merits and faults of Cornelian tragedy were again best summed up by D'Aubignac: Although Corneille often described noble and extraordinary sentiments, created characters whose nobility of soul and forcefulness of purpose evoke our admiration, and sometimes treated passions with great sensitivity, he nonetheless often violated the rules of verisimilitude:

> . . . il s'est relâché souvent en des sentiments peu raisonnables, a introduit des passions nouvelles et peu théâtrales, et souffert des vers rudes, chargés d'obscurité et de façons de parler peu françaises.[49]

D'Aubignac's charge that Corneille's theater lacked uniformity was seconded by La Bruyère:

> Corneille ne peut être égalé dans les endoits où il excelle: il a pour lors un caractère original et inimitable; mais il est inégal.[50]

On the other hand, one of Corneille's most fervent admirers in the second half of the century was Mme de Sévigné, who, unlike most of the critics of the period, judged Cornelian tragedy somewhat apart from the strictest pre-

---

[48] Cf. *op. cit.,* Preface to *Sophonisbe,* II, 771.

[49] Cited in R. Bray, *La Tragédie Cornélienne devant la Critique Française,* p. 4.

[50] *Op. cit.,* p. 82.

cepts of the classical doctrine. Her letters indicate an almost blind admiration for *le grand Corneille*,[51] and it was this fervor that partly prevented her from appreciating the merits of Racinian tragedy.[52] It was also characteristic of her own temperament that she subjected love to "nobler" sentiments:

> Racine fait des comédies pour la Champmeslé: ce n'est pas pour les siècles à venir. Si jamais il n'est plus jeune, et qu'il cesse d'être amoureux, ce ne sera plus la même chose. Vivre [sic] donc notre vieil ami Corneille! Pardonnons-lui de méchants vers, en faveur des divins et sublimes beautés qui nous transportent. . . .[53]

Mme de Sévigné's letters do not, however, present profound analyses of any of Corneille's or Racine's plays; they reveal, rather, her admiration for the lofty sentiments of Corneille and a lack of sympathy for Racine's concern with human passions.

Mme de Sévigné characterized most of Corneille's plays by declaring that the grandeur of the sentiments and the nobility of the characters transported the spectator and caused him to admire the hero. In his Preface to *Médée*, Corneille stated that although Médée was not virtuous and her actions were far from exemplary, one could still admire her forcefulness and determination of purpose. This same view was reflected in his *Discours du Poème Drama-*

---

[51] "Je suis folle de Corneille; il nous redonnera
    Encore Pulchérie, où l'on verra encore
        La main qui crayonne
    La mort du grand Pompée et l'amour de Cinna.
    Il faut que tout cède à son génie."

(*Lettres de Mme de Sévigné* [12 vols.; Paris: Hachette, 1862], *Lettre à Mme de Grignan* 9 mars 1672, II, 259.)

[52] Cf. *ibid., Lettre à Mme de Grignan* 16 mars 1672, III, 535.

[53] *Ibid.*

tique[54] and in his Preface to *Nicomède*, where he explained his theory of admiration:

> Ce héros de ma façon sort un peu des règles de la tragédie, en ce qu'il ne cherche point à faire pitié par l'excès de ses infortunes: mais le succès a montré que la fermeté des grands coeurs, qui n'excite que de l'admiration dans l'âme du spectateur, est quelquefois aussi agréable que la compassion que notre art nous ordonne d'y produire par la représentation de leurs malheurs.[55]

Thus in maintaining that the spectator's admiration for the hero is as valid a means of helping him rid himself of evil passions as is Aristotle's theory of catharsis, Corneille disclosed that the evocation of admiration was the motivating principle of his theater.[56]

Saint-Evremond, one of the most judicious critics of the seventeenth century, was still another fervent admirer of Corneille. While he spent most of his life in England, he was in constant contact with new developments in France and his exile permitted him to view literary developments with more detachment than the critics in France, who were under the direct influence of the new doctrines. His writings indicate a definite preference for Corneille, although, unlike Mme de Sévigné, he also appreciated Racinian tragedy.[57] Saint-Evremond's conception of dramatic art was somewhat similar to Corneille's and one may wonder whether his theory took form before he read Corneille or after. Corneille's opinion that the subject of a tragedy should be both grandiose and extraordinary was approved by Saint-Evremond, who said that in a tragedy

> . . . il faut nous contenter de choses purement naturelles, mais extraordinaires, et choisir, en nos héros, des actions principales

---

[54] Cf. p. 25, n. 32, above.
[55] *Op. cit.,* II, 390.
[56] Cf. *ibid.,* I, 86.
[57] Cf. *op. cit.,* p. 135.

qui soient reçues dans notre créance, comme humaines, et qui nous donnent de l'admiration comme rares et élevées au dessus des autres. En deux mots, il ne nous faut rien que de grand, mais d'humain: dans l'humain, éviter le médiocre: dans le grand, le fabuleux.[58]

It has already been indicated that Corneille was often criticized for his treatment of love, which he considered was not a noble enough passion upon which to base a tragedy. Because of his own temperament, Saint-Evremond, like Mme de Sévigné, was disinclined to elevate love to the rank of a noble passion and thus he too supported Corneille's treatment of this sentiment:

Aux sujets véritablement héroïques, la grandeur d'âme doit être ménagée devant toutes choses. Ce qui serait doux et tendre dans la maîtresse d'un homme ordinaire, est souvent faible et honteux dans l'amante d'un héros . . . elle doit toujours demeurer maîtresse de ses sentiments passionnés, et animer son amant aux grandes choses par sa résolution, au lieu de l'en détourner par sa faiblesse.[59]

It was as a result of such attitudes that the loftiness and nobility of Corneille's plays appealed to Saint-Evremond, who considered the desire to evoke the spectator's admiration an excellent principle upon which to formulate tragedy.[60] Although Saint-Evremond preferred Corneille to Racine, he did not consider Corneille superior to Racine,[61]

---

[58] *Ibid.,* p. 109.

[59] *Ibid.,* p. 145.

[60] ". . . on doit rechercher à la tragédie, devant toutes choses, une grandeur d'âme bien exprimée, qui excite en nous une tendre admiration. Il y a dans cette sorte d'admiration quelque ravissement pour l'esprit; le courage y est élevé, l'âme est touchée." (*Ibid.,* p. 118.)

[61] "In Tragedy *Corneille* admits of no equal, *Racine* of no superior; the diversity of Characters allowing a concurrence, if it cannot establish an equality. . . ." (*The Letters of Saint-Evremond,* ed. J. Hayward [London: Routledge and Sons, 1930], p. 298.)

and concluded with D'Aubignac and La Bruyère[62] that while Cornelian tragedy often portrayed beautiful and admirable sentiments, it sometimes lacked uniformity.[63]

After the quarrel of *le Cid*, Corneille remained in Rouen for four years, whereupon his silence on literary matters and his failure to present another play intrigued his friends and adversaries alike. Although it is not known exactly when and in what theater *Horace* was first presented, it is generally agreed that it was sometime during the year 1640, since the play was printed at the beginning of 1641. According to Corneille the play was well received by the critics.[64] As a matter of fact, very likely as a result of his problem with *le Cid*, *Horace* evinces Corneille's endeavor to follow most scrupulously the rules of the classical doctrine. The critics generally agreed that, unlike *le Cid*, *Horace* not only did not violate the rules of verisimilitude and *bienséance*, but carefully observed the unities of time and place. Their only reproach was that the murder of Camille weakened the unity of action; consequently they condemned Act V on the ground that it was not necessary to the play. Even Corneille conceded that Camille's murder weakened the play.[65] That was the century's only major criticism of *Horace*, which was not always so readily approved of by critics of later periods.

Towards the end of the year in which *Horace* was first performed, Paris witnessed the representation of *Cinna*. The play was warmly received by the critics, who commented that it followed the precepts of dramatic doctrine even more closely than did *Horace*; moreover, *Cinna* was not censured for failing to observe the code of verisimili-

---

[62] Cf. nn. 49, 50, above.

[63] Cf. *op. cit.*, p. 237.

[64] Cf. *op. cit., Examen d'Horace,* p. 832.

[65] Cf. *ibid.,* p. 833.

tude and *bienséance*. According to Balzac, contemporary critics considered Emilie the principal character:

> Emilie inspire, en effet, toute la conjuration, et donne chaleur au parti par le feu qu'elle jette dans l'âme du chef. Elle entreprend, en se vengeant, de venger toute la terre: elle veut sacrifier à son père une victime qui seroit trop grande pour Jupiter même.[66]

Emilie was called one of the two most beautiful Cornelian creations, the other being Sabine:

> Et qu'est-ce que la sainte antiquité a produit de vigoreux et de ferme dans le sexe foible qui soit comparable à ces nouvelles héroïnes que vous avez mises au monde. . . .[67]

Balzac's remark that Emilie is the principal character of the play, and his interpretation of Cinna, whom he considered an *honnête homme* because of his attempt to overthrow a tyrant,[68] reflected current opinion. The succeeding chapters will show that these two opinions were not necessarily held by later critics.

In 1548 the Parlement of Paris had prohibited the representation of mystery plays, and throughout the seventeenth century few important tragedies were based on a religious theme. Of those few the most notable were Corneille's *Polyeucte* and *Théodore,* Du Ryer's *Saül,* and Racine's *Esther,* none of which, except perhaps *Esther,* were at the time considered successful. It was generally agreed that religion was not a proper subject for the theater, and *Polyeucte* was severely criticized for its portrayal of divine together with human love. It is reported that those present at the Hôtel de Rambouillet to whom Corneille gave a reading of *Polyeucte* before its first performance suggested that he

---

[66] Cited in Voltaire, *Commentaires sur Corneille* (Paris: Firmin Didot, 1862), p. 107.

[67] *Ibid.*

[68] Cf. *ibid.,* p. 106.

withdraw it from the repertory of the Hôtel de Bourgogne, where it was to be presented.[69] Boileau also affirmed that religious subjects were inappropriate for the theater:

> De la foi d'un chrétien les mystères terribles
> D'ornemens égayés ne sont point susceptibles :
> L'Evangile à l'esprit n'offre de tous côtés
> Que pénitence à faire, et tourmens mérités ;
> Et de vos fictions le mélange coupable
> Même à ses vérités donne l'air de la fable.[70]

This view, reflecting as it did the doctrine of the times, was maintained by Saint-Evremond:

> L'esprit de notre religion est directement opposé à celui de la tragédie. . . . ce qui eût fait un beau sermon faisait une misérable tragédie. . . .[71]

Polyeucte nonetheless appealed to the spectators and critics who considered Pauline's conflict between her love for Sévère and her duty towards her husband the most touching and important aspect of the play.[72] Mme la Dauphine's opinion that Pauline did not love her husband, but remained faithful to him out of a sense of conjugal duty[73]

---

[69] "Et quelques jours plus tard, alors que Corneille se dispose à traiter avec les comédiens de l'Hôtel de Bourgogne, il voit se présenter chez lui Voiture, fort embarrassé de la démarche dont on l'a chargé. Car l'Hôtel de Rambouillet définitivement désapprouve la tragédie du bon homme. Le mélange d'amour profane et de religion qu'elle contient choque et confond les âmes pieuses. Godeau, consulté, condamne l'auteur assez audacieux pour porter au théâtre une matière sacrée." (Emile Magne, *Voiture et l'Hôtel de Rambouillet* [2 vols.; Paris: Garnier, 1911], II, 229.)

[70] *Op. cit.,* p. 177.

[71] *Op. cit.,* p. 108.

[72] Cf. *ibid.,* pp. 108-109.

[73] "Madame la Dauphine disoit l'autre jour, en admirant Pauline de *Polyeucte:* eh bien! voilà la plus honnête femme du monde qui n'aime point du tout son mari." (De Sévigné, *op. cit., Lettre à Mme de Grignan* 28 août 1680, III, 43.)

summed up the attitude of the period. Incidentally, later-day critics have interpreted *Polyeucte* in a manner that is an almost complete reversal of the seventeenth-century attitude.

In summary it may be said that seventeenth-century critics recognized in Corneille's plays an originality and a grandeur of sentiment that were lacking in the theater before his time. His greatest fault, according to the critics, was that many of his plays did not seem plausible and often violated acceptable social ethics as well as specific rules of drama. In spite of these criticisms Corneille, before 1660, was *le grand Corneille* and there were few dramatists who could be compared to him. After 1660 Corneille's popularity began to decline, not only because he found it increasingly difficult to accommodate his plays to the precepts of the new doctrine, but also because his concern with the heroic and his treatment of love were out of harmony with a temper whose major interest was in the very sentiment Corneille always relegated to second place. Racine's popularity, on the other hand, rose because his theater more closely interpreted changing ideas and interests.

The precepts that regulated dramatic theory in the eighteenth century were essentially the same as those that had governed the art of tragedy in the seventeenth. Even those authors who were the most outspoken in their social and political criticisms generally remained faithful to the basic dramatic principles that had been imposed during the reign of Louis XIV. At the beginning of the eighteenth century Corneille and Racine were the models of classical tragedy, but with the passage of time Cornelian tragedy on the whole was increasingly declared outmoded and incompatible with the interests of the period. There is little information about the attitude of this era towards Corneille; one gains the impression that he probably was read with more veneration than pleasure.

The only major work on Corneille in the first half of the eighteenth century was Voltaire's *Commentaires sur Corneille*, which was not published until 1764. Although he ostensibly wrote the *Commentaires* to praise Corneille, Voltaire continued the denigration of Cornelian tragedy by consistently ranking it below Racinian tragedy. At the end of the eighteenth century La Harpe published his *Cours de Littérature Ancienne et Moderne* (which incidentally was the first consistent history of literature to appear in France).[74] Greatly influenced by Voltaire, La Harpe also endeavored to prove the superiority of Racine over Corneille.

Voltaire analyzed all of Corneille's plays, but he made only a few general remarks about each one and then presented very detailed criticisms of Corneille's style and vocabulary, which he considered inferior to Racine's.[75] Voltaire's hostility towards Corneille and his definite preference for Racine were founded primarily upon the reasons that had caused most of Corneille's difficulty during the latter half of the seventeenth century. Since Voltaire and the dramatists of his era accepted the tenets of the classical doctrine as their guide, it was inevitable that they should find Cornelian tragedy defective. The concern of Voltaire's age with descriptions and analyses of love was more in accord with the temper of their immediate predecessors than was Corneille's concern with the heroic and grandiose:

> . . . je crois que les combats du coeur sont toujours plus intéressants que des raisonnements politiques et ces contestations, qui

---

[74] La Harpe's *Lycée* or *Cours de Littérature Ancienne et Moderne* was first published in 1799.

[75] ". . . il ne faut pas s'attendre à trouver dans Corneille la pureté, la correction, l'élégance du style; ce mérite ne fut connu que dans les beaux jours du siècle de Louis XIV." (*Op. cit.,* p. 87.)

au fond sont souvent un jeu d'esprit assez froid. C'est au coeur qu'il faut parler dans une tragédie.[76]

Corneille had declared that one of his chief aims was to evoke the spectator's admiration for the hero.[77] This principle of Corneille's dramatic doctrine was generally well received by seventeenth-century critics; Voltaire, however, because of his preference in drama for subjects that touched the heart, considered admiration a rather sterile sentiment:

L'admiration n'émeut guère l'âme, ne la trouble point. C'est de tous les sentiments celui qui se refroidit le plus tôt.[78]

Although La Harpe did say that the spectator was often moved by admiration for the Cornelian hero,[79] he supported Voltaire's claim that love was a more interesting and touching sentiment:

. . . l'admiration refroidit souvent le spectateur après l'avoir transporté, l'amour l'émeut et l'intéresse toujours. . . .[80]

Thus Voltaire and La Harpe were unable to accept what Corneille had stated to be a principal motivating element of his theater.

In spite of his criticisms of Cornelian tragedy, Voltaire appreciated *le Cid* because of all of Corneille's plays it was to him the only one that portrayed

---

[76] *Ibid.*, p. 122.

[77] Cf. p. 32, above.

[78] *Op. cit.*, p. 387.

[79] "L'effet des pièces de Corneille est moins touchant, moins profond, moins soutenu, moins déchirant, que celui des pièces de Racine et de Voltaire; mais il est quelquefois plus vif: il arrache moins de larmes, mais il excite plus de transports; car les transports sont proprement l'effet de l'admiration . . . les pièces de Corneille ne serrent pas le coeur; elles élèvent l'âme. . . ." (La Harpe, *Cours de Littérature Ancienne et Moderne* [3 vols.; Paris: Firmin-Didot, 1851], I, 592.)

[80] *Ibid.*

> . . . ce combat des passions qui déchire le coeur, et devant lequel toutes les autres beautés de l'art ne sont que des beautés inanimées.[81]

Admitting that Voltaire was in accord with most of the basic tenets of the classical doctrine as applied to the theater, his ideas on *bon goût* and *bienséance* were not the same as those that had prevailed during the seventeenth century. Voltaire did not consider *le Cid* immoral in terms of social ethics; as a matter of fact, he defended it against the seventeenth-century charge that it was not plausible and that it violated the rules of *bon goût* because Chimène consented to marry Rodrigue:

> . . . et quand on songe que ce mariage est un point d'histoire célèbre, on ne peut que louer Corneille d'avoir réduit ce mariage à une simple promesse d'épouser Chimène; c'est en quoi il me semble que Corneille a observé les bienséances beaucoup plus que ne le pensaient ceux qui n'étaient pas instruits de l'histoire.[82]

Voltaire also defended *le Cid* against Chapelain's charge that the play violated the social code because it illustrated the triumph of love over duty:

> Aimer le meurtrier de son père, et poursuivre la vengeance de ce meurtre, était une chose admirable. Vaincre son amour eût été un défaut capital dans l'art tragique qui consiste principalement dans les combats du coeur; mais l'art était inconnu alors à tout le monde, hors à l'auteur. [83]

La Harpe also admired *le Cid* because, in his opinion, it illustrated the triumph of love over duty and, like Voltaire, he defended the play against the seventeenth-century charge

---

[81] *Op. cit.,* p. 22.

[82] *Ibid.,* p. 24.

[83] Voltaire, *Le Siècle de Louis XIV* (2 vols.; Paris: Garnier, 1947), II, 123.

that it violated the rules of *bienséance*.[84] It should be pointed out that after Voltaire's and La Harpe's defense of the play, *le Cid* was no longer judged against the precepts of verisimilitude and *bienséance*.

Not only do Voltaire's ideas on *le Cid* differ from those of the preceding century; his analysis of *Cinna* contrasts markedly with Balzac's statement that Cinna was generally considered the *honnête homme* of the play.[85] Voltaire observed that at the beginning of the play "on détestait Auguste; on s'intéressait beaucoup à Cinna" and that by Act III, "c'est Cinna qu'on hait, c'est en faveur d'Auguste que le coeur se déclare."[86] Voltaire's contention that Cinna is not the *honnête homme* of the play was supported by La Harpe:

Concluons que le rôle de Cinna est essentiellement vicieux, en ce qu'il manque à la fois, et d'unité de caractère et de vraisemblance morale. . . . N'a-t-il pas fait le rôle d'un malhonnête homme quand il s'est jeté aux genoux d'Auguste pour le déterminer à garder l'empire? Et qui l'obligeait à tant d'hypocrisie? On n'en conçoit la raison, et il paraissait bien plus simple de

---

[84] "Pour condamner le sujet du *Cid,* l'Académie se fonde sur ce qu'il est *moralement invraisemblable* que Chimène consente à épouser le meurtrier de son père le même jour où il l'a tué . . . D'abord il n'est pas vrai que Chimène consente expressément à épouser Rodrigue. Le spectateur voit bien qu'elle y consentira un jour, et il le faut pour qu'il emporte cette espérance, qui est la suite et le complément de l'intérêt qu'il a pris à leur amour. . . . Il est de plus intéressant, puisqu'il excite à la fin l'admiration et la pitié: l'admiration pour Rodrigue, qui ne balance pas à combattre le comte, dont il adore la fille; l'admiration pour Chimène, qui poursuit la vengeance de son père en adorant celui qui l'a tué; et la pitié pour les deux amants, qui sacrifient l'intérêt de leur passion aux lois de l'honneur. . . . Voilà donc l'Académie qui approuve ce qui est vraiment le sujet de la pièce, l'amour combattu par le devoir." (*Op. cit.,* I, 474.)

[85] Cf. p. 35, above.

[86] *Commentaires sur Corneille,* p. 123.

laisser cette bassesse hypocrite à Maxime, qui n'est dans la pièce
qu'un personnage entièrement sacrifié.[87]

La Harpe wrote that although Cinna, the apparent hero
of the play, is dishonest and cowardly, *Cinna* is generally
considered one of Corneille's masterpieces because of the
role of Auguste:

> Le pardon généreux d'Auguste, les vers qu'il prononce, qui sont
> le sublime de la grandeur d'âme; ces vers que l'admiration a
> gravés dans la mémoire de tous ceux qui les ont entendus, et cet
> avantage attaché à la beauté du dénoûment, de laisser au spec-
> tateur une dernière impression qui est la plus heureuse et la plus
> vive de toutes celles qu'il a reçues, ont fait regarder assez
> généralement cette tragédie comme le chef-d'oeuvre de Cor-
> neille. . . .[88]

Voltaire's interpretations of *Horace* and *Polyeucte* were
essentially the same as those of the seventeenth century. He
supported the seventeenth-century criticism that although
Horace followed most of the rules of the classical doctrine,
Camille's murder violated the unity of action.[89] While La
Harpe agreed that *Horace* violated the unity of action,[90]
his analysis of the role of the elder Horace may be considered an indication of how several nineteenth-century
critics[91] were to interpret the play:

> C'est ce rôle étonnant et original du vieil Horace, c'est le beau
> contraste de ceux d'Horace le fils et de Curiace, qui produit
> tout l'effet de ces trois premiers actes; ce sont ces belles créations
> du génie de Corneille qui couvrent de leur éclat les défauts mêlés
> à tant de beautés, et qui, malgré le hors-d'oeuvre absolu des deux

---

[87] *Op. cit.,* I, 488.
[88] *Ibid.,* p. 483.
[89] Cf. *Commentaires sur Corneille,* p. 100.
[90] Cf. *op. cit.,* p. 478.
[91] Lemaître and Faguet in particular.

derniers actes, et la froideur inévitable qui en résulte; malgré le meurtre de Camille, si peu tolérable et si peu fait pour la scène, y conservant toujours cette pièce, moins comme une belle tragédie que comme un ouvrage qui, dans plusieurs parties, fait honneur à l'esprit humain, en montrant jusqu'où il peut s'élever sans aucun modèle et par l'élan de sa propre force.[92]

The seventeenth century was almost unanimous in objecting to the religious theme in *Polyeucte* on the ground that it was not proper to portray divine and human love in the same play.[93] Voltaire's *Zaïre* also portrayed divine and human love, but it expressed the author's anti-religious ideas by illustrating the disastrous consequences of religious fanaticism. *Polyeucte*, on the other hand, showed the beneficial effects of divine grace and undoubtedly that was why Voltaire omitted all reference to it in his *Commentaires*. La Harpe, however, was cognizant of the importance of the religious theme in *Polyeucte*:

Personne n'ignore que le christianisme, qui fait le fond de cet ouvrage, était une des choses qui l'avaient fait condamner par l'Hôtel de Rambouillet.[94]

Voltaire's comments on *Polyeucte* reflected the seventeenth-century judgment that Pauline's love for Sévère and her dilemma between this love and her duty towards Polyeucte was the most interesting element of the play[95] and that while Pauline remained faithful to her husband, her love for Polyeucte was based solely upon her sense of duty.[96] La Harpe also supported most seventeenth-century critics:

---

[92] *Op. cit.,* p. 480.

[93] Cf. p. 36, above.

[94] *Op. cit.,* p. 490.

[95] Cf. *Commentaires sur Corneille,* p. 146.

[96] "N'est-ce point qu'on sent que Pauline n'agit que par devoir, et qu'elle s'efforce d'aimer un homme pour lequel elle n'a point d'amour?" (*Ibid.,* p. 178.)

Pauline . . . emploie pour sauver son mari l'amant qu'elle lui préfère au fond du coeur. . . .[97]

Polyeucte est sur le point d'être conduit à la mort s'il ne renonce point au christianisme. Les larmes de Pauline n'ont pu rien sur lui. Elle s'adresse, pour le sauver, à celui même qui est le plus intéressé à ce qu'il meure, à son rival, à celui qu'elle aime encore, et à qui elle l'a même avoué. . . .[98]

While Voltaire's analysis of *Polyeucte* was concerned primarily with Pauline's love for Sévère and her duty towards Polyeucte, La Harpe's discussion of the play was devoted almost entirely to an examination of the role of Félix. La Harpe censured *Polyeucte* because the denouement depended upon the decision of a character who was neither tragic nor dignified:

Il s'agit de savoir si Félix fera mourir un des personnages les plus importants de la pièce, s'il enverra son gendre à l'échafaud. Il y répugne, car on ne le point ni cruel ni fanatique. Quel est donc le contre-poids qui le fera pencher vers la rigueur? Il n'y en a point d'autre que le calcul erroné d'une très-mauvaise et très lâche politique, et la possibilité très-incertaine de perdre le gouvernement d'Arménie. Ce n'est pas là un ressort suffisant pour la tragédie, où il faut toujours que chaque personnage ait un degré d'intérêt proportionnel, relativement à l'intérêt général.[99]

Notwithstanding that Félix is a weak and cowardly character, I believe that he is a tragic character because of his very weakness and cowardice. Whether his motives are noble or not matters little to the play. The role of Félix is merely a device for creating a situation. However just La Harpe's observation may be, one wonders whether it is im-

[97] *Op. cit.,* p. 592.
[98] *Ibid.,* p. 491.
[99] *Ibid.,* p. 492.

portant enough to warrant basing a lengthy discussion and an analysis of a play on a secondary role.

Voltaire's general opinion of Cornelian tragedy was succinctly resumed in his commentary on *Bérénice*, that although Corneille's plays contained many beautiful elements, they were usually badly conceived and lacking in interest.[100] As would be expected, La Harpe's judgment of Cornelian tragedy was similar:

> Corneille avait une trempe d'esprit naturellement vigeureuse, et une imagination élevée. Le raisonnement, les pensées, les grands traits d'éloquence, dominent dans sa composition; . . . il a donné le premier modèle de ceux qui tiennent à l'élévation de l'âme et des idées, à la force des combinaisons, et il a eu les défauts qui en sont voisins. . . . Comme Lucain, l'amour du grand le conduit jusqu'à l'enflure; comme Sénèque, il fut raisonneur jusqu'à la subtilité et la sécheresse; comme les tragiques espagnols, il força les vraisemblances pour obtenir des effets.[101]

In spite of the efforts of Voltaire and other dramatists of his age to preserve the traditions of classical tragedy, French tragedy in the second half of the eighteenth century was impoverished and flaccid. The classical doctrine had attained its purest expression with the advent of Racinian tragedy. Once created, that genre was faced with serious perils that the dramatists of the eighteenth century were unable to overcome. Classical tragedy imposed strict limitations, the earliest dramatists employing those situations and characters that seemed to be the truest, the most beautiful, the most striking, and the most natural. The successors of

---

[100] "Finissons nos remarques par respect pour Corneille: rendons lui justice; convenons que c'est un grand homme, qui fut trop souvent différent de lui-même, sans que ses pièces malheureuses fissent tort aux beaux morceaux qui sont dans les autres." (*Commentaires sur Corneille*, p. 537.)

[101] *Op. cit.*, p. 588.

Corneille and Racine found it more and more difficult to contain their plays within the classical limits and at the same time avoid repeating situations and conflicts that were becoming a bore to the public. In order to refurbish well-worn material they portrayed the most bizarre ideas and situations,[102] founded, according to Grimm, upon pure fantasy and regulated by a system based on outmoded conventions.[103]

Not only that; but the subjects of drama no longer accorded with the social, religious, and political ideas of a public that had radically changed since the reign of Louis XIV.[104] The dramatists' desire to please and amuse was relegated to second place while moral instruction became the principal aim of the theater. Political, social, and religious propaganda, which had surreptitiously found its way into tragedy in the time of Voltaire, now became the principal object, the *raison d'être*, of the theater. The second half of the eighteenth century witnessed the birth of a new dramatic form, which, created in opposition to classical tragedy, interpreted, rather, the aspirations of the bourgeois, who wished to see situations identifiable with their own daily life.

This new conception of drama was promoted by Diderot and Beaumarchais and designated the *drame sérieux*, or *drame bourgeois*. Beaumarchais complained that the subjects of classical tragedy (which he termed *la tragédie héroïque*) did not interest the public of his era:

Que me font à moi, sujet paisible d'un Etat Monarchique du

---

[102] Cf. E. Caro, *La Fin du dix-huitième Siècle* (Paris: Hachette, 1880), pp. 278-285.

[103] Cf. Félix Gaiffe, *Le Drame en France au XVIIIe Siècle* (Paris: Armand Colin, 1907), pp. 18-20.

[104] Cf. *ibid.*, pp. 77-79.

dix-huitième siècle, les révolutions d'Athènes ou de Rome?[105]

He declared that the situations portrayed by classical tragedy were so far removed from the customs of the day and the characters, mainly kings and princes, so foreign to the average spectator's civil status that they held no interest for the spectator except perhaps to console him for his mediocrity by showing him that great crimes and great misfortunes ordinarily happen only to those who rule the world.[106] If we do find classical tragedy interesting it is not because it touches our heart, but because it excites our vanity:

> . . . examinons quelle espèce d'intérêt les Héros et les Rois, proprement dit, excitent en nous dans la Tradgédie Héroïque, et nous reconnaîtrons peut-être que ces grands événements, ces personnages fastueux, qu'elle nous présente, ne sont que des pièges tendus à notre amour-propre, auxquels le coeur se prend rarement. C'est notre vanité qui trouve son compte à être initiée dans les secrets d'une Cour superbe, à entrer dans un Conseil qui va changer la face d'un Etat, à percer jusqu'au Cabinet d'une Reine dont la vue du trône nous serait permise à peine.[107]

He contended that the only sentiment classical tragedy evoked in the spectator was admiration, which he insisted was a sterile sentiment and unable to move the heart.[108] Thus Beaumarchais, like Voltaire and La Harpe, condemned a major element of Cornelian tragedy.

For these reasons, said Beaumarchais, classical, or heroic, tragedy did not appeal to the spectator who, seeing

---

[105] Beaumarchais, *Théâtre Complet* (Paris: Gallimard, 1949), *Essai sur le Drame,* p. 18.

[106] Cf. *ibid.,* pp. 18-20.

[107] *Ibid.,* p. 18.

[108] Cf. *ibid.,* p. 17.

L'Enfant Prodigue, Nanine, Mélandre, le Père de Famille,
and *Le Philosophe sans le savoir,* was moved by "la peinture touchante d'un malheur domestique,"[109] which was more
powerful than the misfortunes depicted by classical tragedy
because it was one to which the spectator was more suscep-
tible:

> Aussi, bien loin que l'éclat du rang augment en moi l'intérêt que
> je prends aux personnages tragiques, il y nuit au contraire. Plus
> l'homme qui pâtit est d'un état qui se rapproche du mien, et plus
> son malheur a de prise sur mon âme.[110]

The *drame sérieux,* which enjoyed considerable success during the second half of the century, was opposed to the very
essence of classical tragedy and hence to Cornelian tragedy.

[109]*Ibid.,* p. 131.
[110] *Ibid.,* p. 18.

CHAPTER TWO

The Cornelian Legend in the Early Nineteenth Century

THE beginning of the nineteenth century witnessed the creation of a new form of drama which critics of the period termed *le drame moderne*, or *drame romantique*. It was outlined in Hugo's Preface to *Cromwell*[1] in which he presented his definition of drama:

> Du jour où le christianisme a dit à l'homme: "Tu es double, tu es composé de deux êtres, l'un périssable, l'autre immortel, l'un charnel, l'autre éthéré, l'un enchaîné par les appétits, les besoins et les passions, l'autre emporté sur les ailes de l'enthousiasme et de la rêverie, celui-ci enfin toujours courbé vers la terre, sa mère, celui-là sans cesse élancé vers le ciel, sa patrie"; de ce jour le drame a été créé. Est-ce autre chose en effet que ce contraste de tous les jours, que cette lutte de tous les instants entre deux principes opposés qui sont toujours en présence dans la vie, et qui se disputent l'homme depuis le berceau jusqu'à la tombe?[2]

Hugo's simple yet penetrating analysis of the vital principle of modern drama might be considered applicable to Cornelian tragedy in the sense that most of Corneille's plays illustrated a struggle between two opposing principles that on the one hand had their roots in mortal man and on the other in the realm of the ideal.

It was clearly for other reasons that Hugo was hostile

---

[1] *Cromwell* was first published in 1827.

[2] Victor Hugo, *Cromwell* (Paris: Flammarion, 1827), Preface, p. 17.

to the seventeenth-century conception of tragedy. Hugo, having divided all poetry or literature into three ages, each with its own mode of expression,[3] felt that modern drama should depict reality. Whereas seventeenth-century classical doctrine was founded upon verisimilitude, the concept of verisimilitude was in no sense identical with Hugo's definition of reality—a definition which emphasized ugliness as well as beauty,[4] and which insisted that the drama must depict such contrast if it is to describe life.[5] Hugo disapproved of seventeenth-century preoccupation with *le beau*, the transformation of reality in order to express the ideal of the period, and the elimination of the ugly and grotesque from all art forms. It was primarily for such reasons that the romantic and the classical concepts of drama, each with its own definition of reality, were incompatible.[6] Hugo's works on the theater disclosed an intense admiration for Shakespeare and, as would be expected, an almost complete passing over of Cornelian tragedy.

----

[3] "Les temps primitifs sont lyriques, les temps antiques sont épiques, les temps modernes sont dramatiques. L'ode chante l'éternité, l'épopée solennise l'histoire, le drame peint la vie. . . . l'ode vit de l'idéal, l'épopée du grandiose, le drame du réel." (*Ibid.,* p. 15.)

[4] ". . . tout dans la création n'est pas humainement *beau* . . . le laid y existe à côté du beau, le difforme près du gracieux, le grotesque au revers du sublime, le mal avec le bien, l'ombre avec la lumière." (*Ibid.,* p. 9.)

[5] Cf. *ibid.,* pp. 13, 17.

[6] Even before Hugo's Preface to *Cromwell,* Stendhal, in 1823, maintained that romantic drama more closely depicts reality than does classical tragedy: "Le *romanticisme* est l'art de présenter aux peuples les oeuvres littéraires qui, dans l'état actuel de leurs habitudes et de leurs croyances, sont susceptibles de leur donner le plus de plaisir possible. Le *classicisme,* au contraire, leur présente la littérature qui donnait le plus grand plaisir possible à leurs arrière-grands-pères." (Stendhal, *Racine et Shakspeare* [2 vols.; Paris: Champion, 1925], I, 39.)

It was not strange either that Lamartine, a leading figure of the romantic movement, did not find it necessary to develop a comparison between the works of Racine and Corneille in order to indicate his preference: to Racine he devoted more than one *entretien*, to Corneille a few lines.[7] Although Corneille's name appeared rather often throughout the *Cours de Littérature*, as often as any well-known poet's, Lamartine did not analyze any of Corneille's works. He said that in contrast to the religious spirit and melodious language of Racine, Corneille's works were characterized by "une langue de héros" and by "l'enflure espagnole."[8] In view of Lamartine's intention to offer *L'Histoire des Girondins* as an example of political morality, it was a little surprising that he did not admire the poet who made such a point of glorifying virtue.

Opposed to Hugo and Lamartine, three major critics of the period, Saint-Marc Girardin, Janin, and Nisard,[9] preferred seventeenth-century tragedy and admired Corneille. In his *Cours de Littérature Dramatique*, published in 1843, Saint-Marc Girardin presented a study of the theater from antiquity to modern times. He attacked romantic literature because he considered it to be founded upon a somewhat dubious morality and to degrade human sentiments.

---

[7] Stendhal, Hugo, and Lamartine generally approved of Racinian tragedy primarily because it depicted both the good and evil consequences of human passion, particularly love. In spite of Racine's observance of the classical doctrine, Stendhal considered him a romantic dramatist: "Je n'hésite pas à avancer que Racine a été romantique; il a donné, aux marquis de la cour de Louis XIV, une peinture des passions, tempérée par *l'extrême dignité* qui alors était de mode: . . ." (*Ibid.*, p. 40.)

[8] Cf. Alphonse de Lamartine, *Cours Familier de Littérature* (28 vols.; Paris: 1856-1869), III, 20-21.

[9] Saint-Marc Girardin, 1801-1873; Janin, 1804-1874; Nisard, 1806-1888.

Nisard, in his *Histoire de la Littérature Française* (1844–1849), sacrificed the Middle Ages and contemporary literature to extol the classical period, which he considered the apogee of civilization. Although Janin generally approved of the innovations of the romantic writers, his *Histoire de la Littérature Dramatique* (1854), as well as his *Rachel et la Tragédie* (1859), indicated, at least for the theater, a definite preference for Corneille and classical tragedy and a censure of the romantic drama.

One of Hugo's major criticisms of seventeenth-century tragedy was that it did not represent truth or nature and that its characters were not true to life.[10] Saint-Marc Girardin, on the other hand, maintained that classical drama was more true to life than romantic drama:

> La première condition de l'émotion dramatique, c'est que la passion qui l'excite soit vraie. Or, au théâtre il n'y a de vrai que ce qui est général et ce que tout le monde ressent. De toutes les passions dramatiques, l'amour n'est la plus touchante que parce qu'elle est la plus générale. . . . Le théâtre ancien prend pour sujet les passions du coeur humain, les plus générales et les plus communes, l'amour, la tendresse maternelle, la jalousie, la colère; et ces passions, qui sont simples de leur nature, il les représente simplement. Le théâtre moderne, au contraire, cherche, en fait de passions, les exceptions et les curiosités avec autant de soin que le théâtre ancien les évitait.[11]

He also contended that Hugo's idea that the drama appealed more to the senses than to the mind was not justifiable:

> L'art ne doit parler qu'à l'esprit; c'est à l'esprit seul qu'il doit donner du plaisir. S'il cherche à émouvoir les sens, il se dégrade.

---

[10] Cf. p. 50, above.

[11] François Saint-Marc Girardin, *Cours de Littérature Dramatique* (5 vols.; Paris: Charpentier, 1868), I, 4-5.

. . . Les arts sont le langage de l'âme. S'ils s'adressent aux sens, ce n'est que pour les rappeler à leur vocation, qui est d'être les instruments des jouissances de l'âme.[12]

Nisard supported the classical interpretation of tragedy by declaring, as Corneille did, that we are moved more by the portrayal of great events that directly affect illustrious persons than by the representation of commonplace occurrences that strike ordinary people.[13] He agreed with Hugo that tragedy should depict life, but contrarily maintained that seventeenth-century tragedy did just that. Yet though he would attribute such a superior concept of tragedy to Corneille, he would seem to imply that the more effective rendition of the theory was illustrated by Racine:

. . . que de justesse dans cette remarque que nous ne sommes touchés des malheurs des princes "qu'autant que nous sommes susceptibles des passions qui les ont fait tomber dans le précipice!" Voilà le secret même de la tragédie; voilà cette ressemblance avec la vie, qui en fait toute la vérité. Voilà par contre la condamnation de tout poème dramatique où l'on met en scène des passions "dont nous ne sommes pas susceptibles." Cette vue supérieure de Corneille, Racine en fera même la règle de son théâtre.[14]

While Hugo believed that Shakespeare was the greatest modern playwright and the model for the romantic drama, Janin assailed the romantics' idealization of Shakespeare, to the benefit of Corneille:

Entre Shakspeare et Corneille, il n'y a pas à hésiter que je

---

[12] *Ibid.,* pp. 9-10.

[13] ". . . nous cherchons l'idéal de la tragédie au-dessus de nos têtes, dans les événements considérables qui affectent directement des personnes illustres. On ne la fait pas descendre impunément jusqu'aux événements et aux moeurs des personnes de condition privée; la tentative n'en a jamais réussi." (Jean Nisard, *Histoire de la Littérature Française* [3 vols.; Paris: Firmin-Didot, 1881], II, 99.)

[14] *Ibid.*

sache: la couronne de ce grand art appartient à Corneille! Sans
doute, il remplit une scène moins vaste que Shakspeare, il s'adresse
à des crimes moins terribles, à des amours plus charmantes, il
remplit moins d'espace, assurément, *dans ce magnifique jardin
de la nature.* En revanche, il a plus d'âme, il a plus de coeur, il
est plus un homme, il est plus un sage, un philosophe, un politique,
un penseur![15]

Besides criticizing classical drama for its separation of
the sublime and the grotesque, which, according to him, re-
sulted in the creation of abstract rather than human characters, Hugo criticized it for failing to recognize the importance of the décor of a play.[16] Realistic décor and local
color were important aspects of any play whose primary
concern was to depict reality:

> . . . on commence à comprendre de nos jours que la localité
> exacte est un des premiers éléments de la réalité. Les personnages
> parlants ou agissants ne sont pas les seuls qui gravent dans l'esprit
> du spectateur la fidèle empreinte des faits. Le lieu où telle
> catastrophe s'est passée en devient un témoin terrible et insépa-
> rable; et l'absence de cette sorte de personnage muet décomplé-
> terait dans le drame les plus grandes scènes de l'histoire.[17]

While supporting Nisard's and Saint-Marc Girardin's claim
that classical tragedy did present real people,[18] Janin assailed the romantics' concern for local color: elaborate décor
was only a vain accessory employed by the romantic dramatist to conceal the weaknesses of his characters.[19] He cen-

---

[15] Jules Janin, *Histoire de la Littérature Dramatique* (6 vols.;
Paris: Lévy, 1854), III, 351.
[16] "Quoi de plus invraisemblable et de plus absurde en effet que
ce vestibule, ce péristyle, cette antichambre, bien banal où nos tragédies
ont la complaisance de venir se dérouler, où arrivent, on ne sait comment, les conspirateurs pour déclamer contre le tyran, le tyran pour
déclamer contre les conspirateurs. . . ." (*Op. cit.,* p. 19.)
[17] *Ibid.,* p. 20.
[18] Cf. p. 52, above.
[19] Cf. *op. cit.,* p. 344.

sured the romantics' preoccupation with local color by maintaining that classical tragedy lacked such details as furniture, costumes, and armor because

> . . . la Tragédie est elle-même une force, une gloire, un ornement, . . . c'est qu'elle vit par elle-même indépendamment des machinistes; c'est que Corneille est son père.[20]

In the first half of the nineteenth century those critics who supported the romantic theory of drama (Hugo, Lamartine, Stendhal), as well as those opposed to it (Janin, Nisard, Saint-Marc Girardin), discussed Cornelian tragedy primarily as it demonstrated, or not, the relative superiority of classical or romantic drama. Although Nisard revered the classical period and clearly indicated his preference for Corneille, he proposed the innovation that an author should be judged in relation to the period in which he wrote:

> Fontenelle a dit "pour juger de la beauté d'un ouvrage, il suffit de le considérer en lui-même; mais pour juger du mérite d'un auteur, il faut le comparer à son siècle"; il aurait dû ajouter: et à ses devanciers. Pour juger du mérite d'un génie créateur, il faut le comparer au chaos d'où sont sorties ses créations. A ce point de vue, il n'y a pas de plus grand nom dans l'histoire de notre littérature que le nom de Pierre Corneille.[21]

Saint-Beuve, one of the most important critics in the first half of the nineteenth century, followed essentially the method outlined by Nisard.[22] He did not separate literary

---

[20] Jules Janin, *Rachel et la Tragédie* (Paris: Amyot, 1859), p. 75.

[21] *Op. cit.*, p. 97.

[22] "L'état général de la littérature au moment où un nouvel auteur y débute, l'éducation particulière qu'a reçue cet auteur, et le génie propre que lui a départi la nature, voilà trois influences qu'il importe de démêler dans son premier chef-d'oeuvre pour faire à chacune sa part, et déterminer nettement ce qui revient de droit au pur génie." (Charles Sainte-Beuve, *Histoire de la Littérature Française* [4 vols.; Paris: La Renaissance du Livre, n.d.], I, 185.)

criticism from the history of a period or from the life of an author. He considered an author not only a soul to study, an artist whose system was to be analyzed, but also a reflection of the moral and philosophical history of the era. Although he opposed all forms of literary dogmatism and his method of criticism remained essentially the same throughout his career, his later works indicated an endeavor not only to locate an author in his time and environment, but also to outline a natural history of humanity by showing the similarities among authors of various periods. His tendency to classify writers by family inclined him towards Taine's *race, milieu, moment* system of criticism.

The methods employed by Saint-Beuve and Nisard were essentially the same in their attempt to assay the importance and innovation of Cornelian tragedy at the time it was written. They employed the same expressions, qualifying Corneille as "le génie créateur" and "le fondateur du théâtre français," but each interpreted Corneille's creative genius in his own way. Nisard attributed to Corneille the creation of a dramatic form that had no prototype and was the product of Corneille's genius:

> Aucun écrivain n'a plus mérité que Corneille le titre de génie créateur. Il est unique dans l'histoire de notre littérature par la prodigieuse distance qu'il y a entre lui et ceux qui le précèdent immédiatement. . . . un abîme sépare Corneille de tout ce qui peut s'appeler le théâtre avant lui. Et peut-être, pour la langue, y a-t-il plus loin de ce grand poète à la meilleure pièce de théâtre antérieure à lui, que de Descartes lui-même aux meilleurs écrivains du commencement du dix-septième siècle. Descartes crée la méthode, et ne fait que régler la langue; Corneille crée la langue et la méthode. Jusqu'à lui, l'histoire du théâtre n'offre que de vains noms, et pas une pièce. Ce grand art, qui n'a pour ainsi dire point de passé, sort consommé de la tête de Corneille.[23]

---

[23] *Op. cit.,* p. 87.

For Sainte-Beuve, on the other hand, Corneille's genius was in transforming what already existed:

> Quand on parle de création à propos du *Cid*, il faut bien s'entendre. *Création*, dans le sens de faire quelque chose de rien et de tout tirer de soi, il n'en saurait être question ici, puisque toute l'étoffe est fournie d'ailleurs: la création de Corneille est et ne saurait être que dans le ménagement habile, dans le travail complexe qu'il a su faire avec une décision hardie et une aisance supérieure. . . . Ce qui est certain et qu'on peut affirmer sans crainte, c'est que Corneille n'a pas copié et qu'il n'a imité qu'en transformant; il a ramassé, réduit, construit; et avec ce qui n'était que matière éparse,—une riche matière—il a fait oeuvre d'art, et d'art français.[24]

Since these various opinions of the early nineteenth-century critics generally concerned Cornelian tragedy only as it illustrated, or not, the relative superiority of classical or of romantic drama, it is only by studying interpretations of *le Cid, Horace, Cinna,* and *Polyeucte* that we can determine whether seventeenth-century interpretations of these plays persisted or were substantially altered in the first half of the nineteenth century. In the seventeenth century the Académie Française condemned *le Cid* for violating the rules of *bienséance*. In the eighteenth century both Voltaire and La Harpe defended the morality of *le Cid* by maintaining that Chimène did not expressly promise to marry Rodrigue. The early nineteenth century did not seem to be greatly concerned with the morality of *le Cid*. Of the critics cited in this chapter, Nisard was the only one to discuss it at length and, like Voltaire and La Harpe, he defended the play against the charge that it violated social ethics:

> Elle [l'Académie Française] condamna Chimène comme une

---

[24] Charles Sainte-Beuve, *Nouveaux Lundis* (Paris: Lévy, 1867), VII, 256.

fille dénaturée. Ce jugement eût été vrai du haut d'une chaire ; d'une compagnie de gens d'esprit, il était excessif. Tout Paris réclama pour la vérité selon la nature humaine, contre la vérité selon les casuistes de Richelieu.[25]

For seventeenth-century critics the subject of the play appeared to be Chimène's conflict between duty and love, and one of their principal objections was that love and not duty triumphed. For eighteenth-century Voltaire and La Harpe also, the play was based upon Chimène's conflict, and in spite of their hostility to Corneille, they admired *le Cid* primarily because love was seen to take precedence over duty. Nineteenth-century Nisard admired *le Cid,* not only because love was given predominance, but because man's conflict between duty and love was a significant reflection of reality :

La lutte de la passion et du devoir, qu'est-ce autre chose en effet que la vie elle-même ?[26]

Ainsi le devoir et la passion se suivent comme l'ombre suit le corps ; ils s'observent, ils se pressent, ils ne se laissent pas respirer. Cette lutte remplit la pièce toute entière ; on ne s'en lasse point, tant cette image de la vie est forte et attachante.[27]

Sainte-Beuve too was aware that the conflict between duty and love was one of the most important elements of the play.[28] And he too admired *le Cid* primarily because it illustrated the ascendancy of love :

[25] *Op. cit.,* p. 109.

[26] *Op. cit.,* p. 104.

[27] *Ibid.,* p. 107.

[28] "Chimène aime plus Rodrigue, non pas quoique, mais parce qu'il a tué son père ; et lui qui sent qu'il a fait ce qu'il a dû, il a conscience du secret de Chimène et d'autant plus d'envie, avec un reste d'espoir, d'être pardonné. Shakespeare n'aurait pas inventé cela ; c'est trop peu naturel ; il y a trop de compartiments, de contradictions subtiles : mais c'est beau, d'un beau qui suppose le chevaleresque et le

Le *Cid* est une pièce de jeunesse, un beau commencement, le commencement d'un homme, le recommencement d'une poésie et l'ouverture d'un grand siècle. Les vers de premier mouvement et d'un seul jet y sortent à chaque pas; c'est grandiose, c'est transportant. Un jeune homme qui n'admirerait pas le *Cid* serait bien malheureux; il manquerait à la passion et à la vocation de son âge. Le *Cid* est une fleur immortelle d'amour et d'honneur.[29]

Although the essence of *le Cid* had usually been assumed to be the conflict between duty and love, Nisard so strongly stressed the importance of this conflict that one might conclude that the very essence of Cornelian tragedy was the representation of man's eternal struggle between duty and passion.

While it cannot be denied that *le Cid* represents such a struggle, *le Cid* and *Horace* are the only two Cornelian plays based upon the conflict between duty and love. Several of Corneille's other plays may appear to be founded upon such a conflict, but the duty involved is one that is usually invented by the characters. This is particularly true of *Polyeucte, Cinna,* and *Bérénice.* The duty involved in *le Cid* and *Horace* is one imposed upon the characters by external circumstances over which they have little or no control. To interpret all of Cornelian tragedy as the representation of the conflict between duty and love, and the triumph of duty, would be misleading.

Horace was censured by seventeenth-century critics because they believed that Camille's murder violated the unity of action. Although Voltaire and La Harpe also criticized the play for that reason, La Harpe said that *Horace* owed all its beauty to the role of the elder Horace.[30] In the nine-

---

point d'honneur du Moyen-Age. Et aussi la partie humaine, éternelle, s'y retrouve: c'est l'amour." (*Nouveaux Lundis,* VII, 279.)

[29] *Ibid.*

[30] Cf. p. 42, above.

teenth century Saint-Marc Girardin also regarded the role
of the elder Horace as the major one of the play and contended that in spite of the elder Horace's resolution to have
his sons fulfill their obligations to Rome, he did not love his
country more than he loved his children:

> Dirons-nous que le vieil Horace aime sa patrie plus qu'il n'aime
> ses enfants? Non . . . mais le vieil Horace n'a pas pour sa patrie
> les mêmes sentiments que pour ses fils: il aime ses enfants avec
> faiblesse et avec émotion, comme nous les aimons tous; mais il
> aime sa patrie avec une fermeté décidée à tout faire et à tout
> souffrir pour elle.[31]

By emphasizing the importance of the role of the elder
Horace, Saint-Marc Girardin reaffirmed a theme first proposed by La Harpe. The following chapter will show that
La Harpe's and Saint-Marc Girardin's thesis was supported
in the latter half of the nineteenth century.

Although *Cinna* was well received by seventeenth-century
critics, the play was censured because it seemed to contain
shifts of interest from one character to another. During the
first three acts our attention is directed towards Cinna;
beginning with Act IV, Auguste seems to be the major role.
(According to Balzac, Cinna was regarded as the *honnête*
homme of the play because of his attempt to overthrow a
tyrant.[32]) In the eighteenth century Voltaire and La Harpe
also criticized the shift of interest in *Cinna* and, contrary to
seventeenth-century opinion, maintained that Cinna was
dishonest and cowardly.[33] In the nineteenth century Janin,
notwithstanding his admiration for Corneille, supported
Voltaire's and La Harpe's criticism of Cinna:

> *Cinna* est un des grands efforts du génie et de la volonté de Cor-

---

[31] *Op. cit.,* p. 144.
[32] Cf. p. 35, above.
[33] Cf. *ibid.,* pp. 41-42.

neille, et pourtant, Corneille a beau faire, il a trouvé là un héros sans honneur et sans grandeur. Que Cinna soit amoureux d'Emilie jusqu'à immoler l'empereur pour obtenir la main de cette terrible maîtresse, on le comprend à peine, mais que pour avoir, à part soi, une bonne raison d'assassiner l'empereur, Cinna se jette aux pieds d'Auguste afin qu'il garde l'empire, voilà ce que je ne saurais bien comprendre. Il y a dans cette action de Cinna un affreux mensonge.[34]

If Cinna is assumed to be a dishonest and cowardly character, who else in the play holds our interest and stimulates our curiosity? It certainly is not Emilie, who, although regarded in the seventeenth century as one of Corneille's most beautiful creations, was in the nineteenth century judged a rather cold and inhuman character.[35] In the nineteenth century La Harpe declared that Auguste was the most beautiful role in *Cinna* and that his pardon of the conspirators was an example of his nobility of soul. Janin sustained La Harpe by proposing that Auguste held one's interest and was the very *raison d'être* of the play:

... le seul héros de ce grand drame et le seul qui joue un grand rôle, le seul qui m'intéresse et m'attire par la beauté, c'est-à-dire, par la constance de son caractère, c'est Auguste ... telle est la force de cet homme, sur lui-même, qu'il va triompher à la fois de ces haines et de sa propre vengeance. Oui, le pardon entier, parti du coeur, venu de l'âme ... irrésistible et vainqueur de toutes les passions vulgaires, va rendre cet homme plus grand même que la possession sans limites du monde connu! Voilà tout le drame et tout l'intérêt de ce drame illustre.[36]

---

[34] *Rachel et la Tragédie,* p. 103.

[35] "Celle-là [Emilie] était bien la plus rancuneuse des créatures, et parfaitement insolente. Chacune de ses paroles est une injure; son geste est insultant, son regard ironique; c'est une femme à n'épouser ses amants que de la main gauche." (*Ibid.,* p. 104.)

[36] *Ibid.,* pp. 106-107.

According to Janin, the role of Auguste depicted the development of a character and was an example of the exercise of will to subjugate the desire for vengeance. Janin indicated that if there was a question of duty in *Cinna,* it was a duty invented by the hero and not, as in *le Cid,* one imposed on the hero by circumstances.[37]

Polyeucte was severely criticized by seventeenth-century critics, who felt that religious subjects were not appropriate for the theater. In the eighteenth century Voltaire also condemned the religious theme in *Polyeucte*; and La Harpe, although he indicated that Polyeucte's martyrdom was the principal element of the play, did not develop this theme.[38] In the nineteenth century Saint-Marc Girardin maintained that the subject of the play was Polyeucte's martyrdom, but, like La Harpe, he did not emphasize that idea.[39] The interpretation of *Polyeucte* as a representation of the early rise of Christianity and of the effect of divine grace was first proposed by Sainte-Beuve:

> Corneille s'était emparé, au passage, de cette idée grondante, de ce coup de foudre de la Grâce, pour s'en faire hardiment un tragique flambeau; ... Il s'était donc mis à saisir, sans plus tarder, cette inspiration nouvelle, cette Grâce (dans toutes les acceptions) dont il sentait sur lui, au dedans de lui, la tentation heureuse; et ce naïf génie, ce franc et noble coeur, s'y appliquant dans toute son ouverteur, en avait dès l'abord atteint et exprimé la profonde science.[40]

While Corneille was only three years old at the time of

---

[37] Cf. *ibid.,* p. 109.

[38] Cf. p. 43, above

[39] "Le martyre de Polyeucte, et par conséquent, l'enthousiasme religieux, voilà le sujet principal de la tragédie. . . . (*Op. cit.,* IV, 444.)

[40] Charles Sainte-Beuve, *Port-Royal* (2 vols.; Paris: Gallimard, 1953), I, 183.

the events of the famous *Journée du Guichet*[41] and in later
life had no direct relations with Port-Royal, Sainte-Beuve
compared *Polyeucte* to the *Journée du Guichet*:

> Que si l'on envisage le côté pathétique et profond, la valeur
> morale de cette scène (du Guichet), la grandeur et la sincérité
> des sentiments en présence, ce combat de la nature et de la Grâce,
> et le triomphe de celle-ci, il me semble qu'il y a sujet de sortir du
> privé et du domestique, et de ce qui n'est que du cloître et de la
> famille Arnauld, d'en sortir, ou plutôt de s'en emparer librement,
> pour embrasser le fond même et la source, pour se porter à toute
> la hauteur des plus dignes comparaisons. J'ai déjà prononcé le
> nom de *Polyeucte*. Le *Polyeucte* de Corneille n'est pas plus beau
> à tous égards que cette circonstance réelle, produite durant le bas
> âge du poète, et il n'émane pas d'une inspiration différente. C'est
> le même combat, c'est le même triomphe; si Polyeucte émeut et
> transporte, c'est que quelque chose de tel était et demeure pos-
> sible encore à la nature humaine secourue.[42]

Sainte-Beuve compared all the characters in *Polyeucte* to
the people who actually took part in the *Journée du Guichet*.
The following was an example:

> Il est vrai que dans l'admirable scène de Polyeucte et de Pauline,
> quand celle-ci essaie de l'ébranler, le héros à un moment s'échappe
> à dire hélas! . . . le moment de cet *hélas*! dans la scène entre
> Pauline et Polyeucte est juste celui de l'évanouissement dans la
> scène entre Angélique et son père. . . .[43]

While seventeenth- and eighteenth-century critics did not

---

[41] One of the measures instituted by la mère Angélique in her
attempt to reform the convent of Port-Royal was the absolute ex-
clusion of all laymen from the convent buildings. The scene that
took place on September 25, 1609, when she refused to permit
her father, M. Arnauld, to enter the convent, is referred to as the
Journée du Guichet.

[42] *Port-Royal,* I, 177.

[43] *Ibid.,* p. 186.

generally approve of the religious implications of *Polyeucte,* it was nonetheless one of Corneille's most successful plays.[44] The audience was more interested in Pauline's conflict between her love for Sévère and her duty towards Polyeucte than in the religious theme. Whether Pauline would marry Sévère or not was the question that interested the spectator the most. It will be recalled that critics during the seventeenth and eighteenth centuries generally considered Pauline an honest and virtuous woman who didn't love her husband; in the nineteenth century Saint-Marc Girardin maintained that although Pauline did not love Polyeucte at the beginning of the play, she did love him at the end:

> Pauline n'aimait pas son mari quand elle l'a épousé. Cependant le devoir, comme cela arrive dans les âmes honnêtes, a créé l'affection, et Pauline maintenant aime Polyeucte, car elle craint pour ses jours et s'alarme du songe qui semble menacer sa vie. Cette affection, née du devoir, peut-elle lutter contre l'inclination qu'elle a eue pour Sévère. Oui, dans l'âme de Pauline, le devoir peut lutter et l'emporter sur l'inclination.[45]

He claimed that Pauline's love for Polyeucte was based upon her sense of duty and honor[46] and concluded that the play represented Pauline's conflict between her love for Sévère and her idea of conjugal duty:

---

[44] From 1680 to 1800 there were 239 performances of *Polyeucte* at the Comédie-Française. Of all Corneille's tragedies only four surpassed *Polyeucte* in the number of performances for the same period: *le Cid,* 479; *Cinna,* 318; *Rodogune,* 314; *Horace,* 272. Cf. A. Joannidès, *La Comédie-Française de 1680 à 1920* (Paris: Plon, 1921).

[45] *Op. cit.,* IV, 407.

[46] "Pauline, en effet, ne représente pas l'amour conjugal: elle n'en a ni l'ardeur, ni la confiance, ni la naïveté. Elle représente l'honneur conjugal; elle en a l'élévation, la pureté, la sévérité." (*Ibid.*)

Pauline représente la lutte du devoir contre la passion.[47]

Sainte-Beuve also declared that Pauline loved Polyeucte at the end of the play, but he did not depict her torn between duty and love:

Pauline n'est pas du tout passionnée dans le sens antique: l'amour, comme elle peut le ressentir, ne rentre pas dans ces maladies fatales, dans ces vengeances divines dont les Didon et les Phèdre sont atteintes: ... Elle n'a pas non plus la *mélancolie* moderne et la rêverie de pensée des Marguerite, des Ophélie. Pauline est précise, elle est sensée. Avant de devenir l'épouse de Polyeucte, elle a aimé Sévère ... dès que le devoir et son père l'ont commandé, elle a rejeté d'elle l'idée de ce *parfait amant*, et a pu être à Polyeucte sans infidélité secrète du coeur, sans souffrance ni flamme cachée.[48]

Sainte-Beuve, like Saint-Marc Girardin, asserted that Pauline's love for Polyeucte was based upon her sense of conjugal duty, but, contrary to the latter, contended that this was the only type of love she was capable of:

La *raison,* qui l'a tirée de son inclination première, l'a conduite à l'affection conjugale. Car, au milieu des exaltations de langage et de croyance, à travers ce songe mystérieux et ces coups de la Grâce, au fond la *raison* règle et commande ce caractère si charmant, si solide et si sérieux de Pauline, une raison capable de tout le devoir dévoué, de tous les sacrifices intrépides, de toutes les délicatesses mélangées; une raison qui, même dans les extrémités les plus rapides, lui conserve une sobriété parfaite d'expression, une belle simplicité d'attitude: tout par héroïsme, rien par entraînement.[49]

---

[47] *Ibid.,* p. 425.
[48] *Port-Royal*, p. 195.
[49] *Ibid.,* p. 196.

CHAPTER THREE

The Legend Modified
in the Late Nineteenth Century

IN the second half of the nineteenth century some critics, particularly Brunetière, Faguet, Lemaître, and Lanson, reevaluated Cornelian tragedy. They sought to determine the principal elements of his theater independently of external circumstances and to modify previous interpretations of his theater as the representation of conflict between duty and passion. The two ideas that appeared most often in their evaluation were that the primary aim of Cornelian tragedy was the glorification of man's will and that its characters believed they were free to choose their course of action and were thus the masters of their destiny.

Brunetière said that the glorification of will and Corneille's desire to evoke the spectator's admiration for the hero were the two major elements of his theater:

> Avouons-le donc une fois, et achevons de le comprendre : ce n'est proprement ni le devoir ni la passion qu'il s'est plu à nous représenter, c'est la volonté, quel qu'en fût d'ailleurs l'objet; et ce n'est ni la pitié, ni la terreur même qu'il s'est proposé d'exciter ou de remuer en nous, c'est l'admiration.[1]

> Mais ce qui est plus vrai, ce qui l'est même absolument, et ce qu'il faut dire, c'est que le théâtre de Corneille est la glorification où l'apothéose de la volonté.[2]

---

[1] Brunetière, *Les Epoques du Théâtre Français* (Paris: Hachette, 1896), p. 76.
[2] Brunetière, *Etudes Critiques sur l'Histoire de la Littérature Française* (Paris: Hachette, 1891), sixième série, p. 120.

Lemaître reinforced Brunetière's contention that Corneille's theater represented the glorification of will[3] and also proposed, in a rather pejorative manner, that the Cornelian hero's desire to dominate his feelings was often the result of pride:

> . . . le culte de la volonté n'est plus alors que le culte de l'orgueil . . . Cet orgueil, cet héroïsme content de soi, ces pétarades de la volonté, cette emphase, cette redondance rempliront tout le théâtre de Corneille. . . .[4]

The Cornelian hero's desire to overcome his sentiments out of the sole desire to be the master of his actions may be true, to some degree, in *Cinna, Tite et Bérénice,* and *Théodore;* but Lemaître maintained that the principal characters in almost all of Corneille's later tragedies were motivated by pride.[5] He made only passing mention of Corneille's desire to excite admiration for the hero and insisted that Corneille's main object was the glorification of will.

Lanson's interpretation of Cornelian tragedy was essentially the same as Lemaître's and Brunetière's:

> Corneille a éclairé toutes ses peintures d'un même jour: il a adopté un parti pris, qui fait l'unité et la plus sensible originalité de son oeuvre. Il a "sa" psychologie singulière et personnelle, un

---

[3] "Corneille, le poète du devoir? Non pas, mais de la volonté. Ce qu'il exalte dans quinze ou vingt drames, c'est le triomphe de la volonté toute seule, ou tout au plus de la volonté appliquée à quelque devoir extraordinaire, inquiétant, atroce . . ." (Lemaître, *Impressions de Théâtre* [Paris: Boivin, 1886-1889], première série, p. 11.)

[4] Lemaître, *Pierre Corneille* in *Histoire de la Littérature Française,* published under the direction of L. Petit de Julleville (Paris: Armand Colin, 1897), IV, 272.

[5] Brunetière supported Lemaître's contention that the Cornelian hero's endeavor to dominate his feelings was often the result of pride. Cf. Brunetière, *Etudes Critiques sur l'Histoire de la Littérature Française,* p. 130.

système à travers lequel il voit la vie, auquel il réduit toutes ses imitations de la vie. Dans tous les facteurs internes de nos actes, il isole un principe; la raison; une force: la volonté; il recherche comment la volonté fait triompher la raison. Dans l'infinité du réel et du possible, il choisit les cas merveilleux où s'exprime la grandeur de la volonté tendue contre les sollicitations du dedans et les pressions du dehors; il déplore la beauté de l'âme libre prolongeant par un fier effort l'idée de sa raison dans son acte . . . Aussi peut-on considérer l'idée de la volonté comme le principe générateur de la tragédie cornélienne.[6]

Brunetière, Lemaître, and Lanson did not support earlier interpretations of Cornelian tragedy as the representation of man's conflict between duty and passion, but they did reinforce their predecessors' view that one of Corneille's principal aims was the glorification of will. While Brunetière and Lemaître declared that the Cornelian hero's endeavor to prove that he was the master of his destiny was often the result of pride, Lanson, on the other hand, maintained that Corneille's characters employed reason to justify their actions and thus attempted to establish relative control over the circumstances with which they were confronted.

One of Corneille's most frequently quoted prefaces was the *Avis* of *Nicomède* in which he said:

Voici une pièce d'une constitution assez extraordinaire: aussi est-ce la vingt et unième que j'ai fait voir sur le théâtre; et après y avoir fait réciter quarante mille vers, il est bien malaisé de trouver quelque chose de nouveau, sans s'écarter un peu du grand chemin, et se mettre au hasard de s'égarer. La tendresse et les passions, qui doivent être l'âme des tragédies, n'ont aucune part en celle-ci: la grandeur du courage y règne seul et regarde son malheur d'un oeil si dédaigneux qu'il n'en saurait arracher une plainte. Elle y est combattue par la politique, et n'oppose à ses artifices qu'une prudence généreuse, qui marche à visage dé-

---

[6] Lanson, *Corneille* (Paris: Hachette, 1898), pp. 74-75.

couvert, qui prévoit le péril sans s'émouvoir, et ne veut point
d'autre appui que celui de sa vertu, et de l'amour qu'elle inspire
dans les coeurs de tous les peuples . . . Dans l'admiration qu'on a
pour la vertu je trouve une manière de purger les passions dont
n'a point parlé Aristote et qui est peut-être plus sûre que celle
qu'il prescrit à la tragédie par le moyen de la pitié et la terreur.[7]

Commenting on the *Avis*, Faguet said that the essence
of Cornelian tragedy was neither the conflict between duty
and passion nor the glorification of will, but the desire to
excite admiration for the hero:

. . . Corneille a trouvé ce qui peut être considéré comme la formule de son théâtre: le pathétique d'admiration.[8]

. . . ce que Corneille veut surtout c'est qu'on admire, qu'on admire ses personnages et qu'on l'admire lui-même, qu'on s'étonne
de voir jusqu'où peut aller la nature humaine dans la véhémence,
soit dans l'outrance de la passion, soit dans l'exaltation d'une
vertu, soit dans la tension exaspérée de la volonté.[9]

He considered the glorification of will only a "cas particulier" of Corneille's desire to stimulate admiration by the
representation of subjects and characters "qui étonnent, qui
enlèvent, qui font frissonner."[10]

Rigal, subscribing to Faguet's thesis, said that Cor-

---

[7] *Oeuvres* (2 vols.; Paris: La Pléiade, 1950), II, 385.
[8] Faguet, *En lisant Corneille* (Paris: Hachette, 1914), p. 182.
[9] *Ibid.,* pp. 97-98.
[10] "Le fond de Corneille, ce n'est pas, comme on le disait du
temps ou pour juger d'un auteur on en lisait cent pages, la lutte de la
passion et du devoir et la victoire de celui-ci; ce n'est pas non plus,
quoique ici nous soyons plus près du vrai, l'exaltation de la volonté;
c'est d'une façon plus générale, le goût des choses "qui étonnent,
qui enlèvent, qui font frissonner" (Mme de Sévigné) et la puissance
de les créer, et la tension formidable de la volonté n'est qu'un *cas
particulier* de cette tendance générale. . . ." (*Ibid.,* p. 183.)

neille's principal aim was to stir our admiration[11] and that
the cult of will was one of the ways by which he excited it.
Although Faguet agreed with Brunetière, Lemaître, and
Lanson that the glorification of will was an important element in Corneille's theater, he considered this to be only
one aspect of Corneille's desire to capture the imagination
of the spectator and evoke his admiration.

Faguet's innovation was that he viewed the cult of will
only as a means to an end and not as an end in itself. A
glance at *Médée*, *Le Cid*, *Horace*, *Cinna*, *Polyeucte*, *Rodogune*, and *Nicomède* showed Corneille's taste for extraordinary subjects, savage passions, and inhuman situations:
Médée killing her two children, Horace stabbing Camille,
Cléopâtre poisoning her son, and Ptolomée presenting
Pompée's head to César. The limitless energy and determination of these characters made them worthy of admiration even when their acts were not commendable.[12]

The two most potent expressions of man's energy are
passion and will. While passion may be considered an expression of energy characterized by undirected or irrational
action, will, on the other hand, is usually interpreted as an
expression of energy controlled and directed by reason.
Lanson maintained that Corneille's heroes believed them-
selves free to choose their course of action, to shape their
destiny:

> Corneille peint des volontés. Ses personnages sont pleinement
> conscients, ils combinent leur action, la choisissent avec connais-
> sance. Ils ne sont pas emportés, traînés: ils se déterminent, ils
> vont d'eux-mêmes. Les données du sujet leur ouvrent une sphère
> d'action, et en même temps la limitent: ils s'y meuvent par leur

---

[11] Cf. Eugène Rigal, *De Jodelle à Molière* (Paris: Hachette,
1911), p. 283.

[12] Corneille indicated this in his *Discours du Poème Dramatique*
when he defended the morality of *Rodogune*. Cf. p. 25, above.

libre arbitre, agissant et réagissant entre eux, et composant un système fermé de forces qui trouve enfin leur arrêt dans le dénouement.[13]

Le théâtre de Corneille est plein de héros appliqués à servir leur passion de toute leur volonté, comme leur passion est appliquée à la légitimer.[14]

Faguet reinforced Lanson's thesis:

Le héros cornélien est tenu pour libre: il n'est pas "déterminé"; il a à savoir ce qu'il doit préférer entre deux avertissements de sa raison et de sa conscience . . . Dans tous les cas, c'est le problème de la liberté ou celui de la responsabilité humaine, le même sous une face ou sous une autre face, qui se pose et qui s'agite. C'est: que pouvons-nous faire? et: Que devons-nous faire? qui est en question.[15]

Ce que Corneille invente, c'est précisement le personnage actif et non passif, qui marche à un but, consulte, résout, achève, qui est l'artisan même de sa destinée. . . . le principal événement, l'événement essentiel de *la pièce*, c'est parbleu, bien lui qui le fait, qui le crée, par un acte de sa puissante volonté, par une *décision* du moi.[16]

Brunetière said that in all the plays before Corneille the action was always caused by external circumstances and that the innovation of *le Cid* was that for the first time

. . . les causes de l'action et l'action même y sont transportées du dehors au dedans; et le drame, par conséquent, s'y déroule dans l'intérieur ou dans l'âme des personnages. Tout ce que sont les personnages de Corneille, ils le sont par eux-mêmes, indé-

---

[13] *Op. cit.,* p. 126.

[14] *Ibid.,* p. 96.

[15] Faguet, *Propos de Théâtre* (première et deuxième série; Paris: Société Française d'Imprimerie et de Librairie, 1903-1905), première série, p. 14.

[16] *Ibid.,* p. 90.

pendamment des événements, ou au besoin contre les événements mêmes. . . . les personnages, au lieu d'être les "produits de leurs propres actions, en deviennent vraiment les maîtres, les vrais ouvriers de leur fortune au lieu de n'en être que les esclaves ou les jouets."[17]

Brunetière, Faguet, and Lanson maintained that the Cornelian hero used reason to justify his acts and thus believed that he shaped his own destiny, even if he had little or no control over the circumstances of his predicament.

It is not always easy to distinguish will from passion in Cornelian tragedy, where limitless will may develop into uncontrollable passion. It is also evident that passion is often accompanied by unbounded determination. If by will is meant self-control necessitated by external obligations (*devoir*), then Cornelian tragedy, except perhaps for *le Cid* and *Horace*, does not represent the glorification of will. If, however, we interpret the term to mean strong purpose and deliberate action, then Cornelian tragedy is based primarily on the glorification of will. Perhaps instead of calling Corneille the poet of will, which seems to imply that his characters are free to choose their course of action, we should call him the poet of unbounded energy and determination, whatever the motivating factors. In many of Corneille's plays determination in the protagonist is motivated by passion: in Médée and Cléopâtre, by hatred; in Polyeucte and Théodore, by religious fervor; in Ptolomée, by fear and ambition; and in Bérénice and Auguste, to some extent by pride. Only in *le Cid* and *Horace* are the principal characters motivated by a duty imposed from the outside, and thus these two plays may be considered exceptions in Corneille's theater.

---

[17] *Les Epoques du Théâtre Français,* p. 16.

The critics mentioned in this chapter agreed that Cornelian tragedy did not always represent the conflict between duty and passion, but their interpretations of individual plays offered striking contrasts. It might be appropriate at this point to analyze *le Cid*, *Horace*, *Cinna*, and *Polyeucte*.

Brunetière, Lemaître, Faguet, Rigal, and Lanson agreed that *le Cid* represented the conflict between duty and passion. So much has been written about this conflict in *le Cid* that to quote any of the aforementioned critics would only be repetitious. Faguet succinctly resumed the generally accepted interpretation of *le Cid*: it was Corneille's first play in which

> ... la lutte de la passion et du devoir est déchaînée et avec une violence extraordinaire; ... et le *Cid* seul des grandes tragédies met aux prises le devoir et la passion, si puissamment du reste et laissant une telle impression sur les esprits que beaucoup ont cru, par paresse du reste à lire et à imaginer, que tout Corneille était là.[18]

While this generally accepted interpretation is somewhat justified, one may question it. Sainte-Beuve, Nisard, and La Harpe indicated that the duty involved in *le Cid* was based upon the *point d'honneur*:[19] Rodrigue, by challenging the Count, upheld his family's honor; Chimène, by seeking vengeance for her father's death, maintained her honor. The *point d'honneur* was an almost inescapable duty for a seventeenth-century French nobleman. Brunetière agreed with Nisard[20] that Corneille's characters created the situations into which they were thrown:

> Ce que l'on imputait au hasard de la rencontre, il en a reporté

---

[18] *En lisant Corneille,* p. 108.
[19] Cf. p. 58, above.
[20] Cf. *ibid.*

l'honneur aux résolutions volontaires de son Rodrigue et de sa Chimène.[21]

This generally accepted interpretation of the conflict involved in *le Cid* is not completely justifiable, because Rodrigue's and Chimène's duty is a real one; it is not one that they invent. Perhaps it is Corneille's talent that conveys the impression they have a choice when in reality they do not. Rodrigue's decision to avenge his father is made in Act I:

> Mourir sans tirer ma raison!
> Rechercher un trépas si mortel à ma gloire!
> Endurer que l'Espagne impute à ma mémoire
> D'avoir mal soutenu l'honneur de ma maison!
> Respecter un amour dont mon âme égarée
>   Voit la perte assurée!
> N'écoutons plus ce penser suborneur,
>   Qui ne sert qu'à ma peine.
> Allons, mon bras, sauvons du moins l'honneur,
> Puisqu'après tout il faut perdre Chimène.[22]

In Act II, Chimène realizes that Rodrigue has no choice and supports his decision:

> S'il ne m'obéit point, quel comble à mon ennui!
> Et s'il peut m'obéir, que dira-t-on de lui?
> Etant né ce qu'il est, souffrir un tel outrage!
> Soit qu'il cède ou résiste au feu qui me l'engage,
> Mon esprit ne peut qu'être ou honteux ou confus,
> De son trop de respect, ou d'un juste refus.[23]

Rodrigue's hesitation lasts for only a few moments because he realizes that he has no choice. Whatever conflict there may be for Rodrigue between duty and love ends with Act I.

---

[21] *Les Epoques du Théâtre Français,* p. 21.
[22] I, 1.
[23] II, 3.

Chimène's decision to avenge her father's death is made with her cry to the king:

Sire, Sire, justice![24]

Chimène, like Rodrigue, has no choice: she must do what the conventions require.

Although Rodrigue and Chimène are torn between their duty and their love, their conflict is one that does not demand a decision. Where there is a struggle between duty and passion such a conflict is essentially terminated once the decision has been made. Rodrigue resolves to fulfill his obligations to his father at the end of Act I. Chimène's resolution to avenge her father's death is made known at the end of Act II. What holds our interest is not what their decision will be, for we know that at the beginning of the play, but their determination to execute their duties. Brunetière indicated this when he said that the spectator's major question was

> . . . jusqu'où peut aller la force de l'amour, et si dans l'âme de Rodrigue elle fera taire la voix de l'honneur, ou si dans le coeur de Chimène elle étouffera celle du sang, voilà le vrai sujet de Corneille.[25]

Their persistence in discharging their obligations to the fullest, in spite of their love, causes us to admire their determination, which, according to Faguet, was Corneille's principal aim.

Rodrigue's victory over the Moors, the Infanta's advice to Chimène, the decision of the king in Act V, all conspire to help liberate Rodrigue and Chimène from fulfilling their obligations. At the end it is not duty but love that tri-

---

[24] II, 8.

[25] *Etudes Critiques sur l'Histoire de la Littérature Française,* p. 110.

umphs. For this reason critics consider *le Cid* an exception or even an accident in Cornelian tragedy. Lemaître supported Faguet's contention[26] that *le Cid* illustrated the triumph of love over duty:

> En sorte que ce qu'il y a au fond du *Cid*, en dépit des discours ininterrompus sur l'honneur et sur le devoir, c'est la proclamation des droits imprescriptibles de l'amour, entendez de l'amour passion. *Le Cid* célèbre, sans en avoir l'air, le triomphe de la nature sur une convention sociale, ou, si vous y tenez, la revanche de l'esprit contre la lettre de la loi.[27]

The idea that all Cornelian tragedy pits duty against passion and that duty triumphs is erroneous. Most critics agree that *le Cid* portrays a conflict between duty and love, but they maintain that love triumphs. It is singular that Corneille's most celebrated play is perhaps the least typical example of Cornelian tragedy.

Horace has usually been termed the poem of patriotism. Faguet clearly resumed this generally accepted idea:

> Il y a à remarquer que Corneille consciemment ou non, y a montré le patriotisme dans toutes ses nuances, depuis le patriotisme combattu par les sentiments de famille dans Curiace, jusqu'au patriotisme n'éteignant pas les sentiments de famille dans le vieil Horace (Moi-même en cet instant j'ai les larmes aux yeux), jusqu'au patriotisme frénétique et exclusif de tout autre sentiment chez Horace le fils, sans compter le personnage naturel, instinctif et impulsif [Camille] qui ne connait pas le patriotisme du tout.[28]

---

[26] "Ce qu'il y a de curieux, c'est que dans la seule tragédie où Corneille ait montré la lutte du devoir contre la passion, ce n'est pas le devoir que finalement il fait triompher. . . ." (*En lisant Corneille,* p. 109.)

[27] *Pierre Corneille,* p. 279.

[28] *En lisant Corneille,* p. 114.

Since *Horace* is Corneille's only play, besides *le Cid*, in which the characters are confronted with a duty over which they have little or no control, seventeenth- and eighteenth-century critics usually interpreted it as the portrayal of conflict between duty and love. Lemaître resumed this generally accepted interpretation thus:

> *Horace* est la seule tragédie de Corneille à laquelle convient exactement les traditionnelles définitions de l'esprit cornélien et dont on puisse dire avec vérité que le devoir y triomphe de la passion . . . Mais dans *Horace*, il s'agit d'un devoir évident, indiscutable, intelligible à tous les hommes: le sacrifice du citoyen à la patrie.[29]

Faguet did not accept this interpretation: in *Horace* there were only

> . . . passions qui ne luttent nullement entre elles (chaque personnage a sa passion qu'il suit tout droit et il n'y a nullement une partie de lui-même qui se batte contre l'autre).[30]

> . . . il n'y a nulle bataille de la passion contre le devoir, mais le choc l'une contre l'autre des deux plus grandes passions qui existent, l'amour et l'amour du pays, et une grande âme déchirée entre son amour pour son pays et son amour pour ses enfants qu'il lui sacrifie.[31]

Although it would appear that Faguet and Lemaître were in complete disagreement on the conflict of duty and passion in *Horace*, both of their interpretations are justifiable. There is in *Horace*, as Lemaître indicated, "un devoir évident, indiscutable"—patriotism, or duty to one's country. The characters of *Horace*, like those of *le Cid*, are confronted with a duty imposed by external circumstances

---

[29] *Impressions de Théâtre*, p. 285.
[30] *En lisant Corneille*, p. 108.
[31] *Ibid.*, p. 96.

over which they have little or no control. In this respect
Lemaître's interpretation is tenable, but there is no conflict
between duty and love within either young Horace, Curiace,
or Camille. The younger Horace does not hesitate to accept his duty:

> Mourir pour le pays est un si digne sort,
> Qu'on briguerait en foule une si belle mort. . . .[32]

Curiace, on the other hand, accepts his duty with regret:

> . . . puisque par ce choix Albe monte en effet
> Qu'elle m'estime autant que vous pour Rome;
> J'ai le coeur aussi bon, mais enfin je suis homme:
> Je vois que votre honneur demande tout mon sang,
> Que tout le mien consiste à vous percer le flanc,
> Près d'épouser la soeur, qu'il faut tuer le frère,
> Et pour mon pays j'ai le sort si contraire.
> Encor qu'à mon devoir je coure sans terreur,
> Mon coeur s'en effarouche, et j'en frémis d'horreur;
> J'ai pitié de moi-même, et jette un oeil d'envie
> Sur ceux dont notre guerre a consumé la vie,
> Sans souhait toutefois de pouvoir reculer.[33]

He is the only character in whom there is a conflict between
duty and love, but Corneille does not develop the conflict
and Curiace does not appear after Act II.

Faguet's contention that Camille was moved only by
her love for Curiace[34] was reinforced by Lemaître:

> . . . Camille est la seule femme de Corneille qui soit enragée de
> passion, et qui sacrifie délibérément son devoir à son amour.[35]

Sarcey also supported this idea:

---

[32] II, 3.
[33] *Ibid.*
[34] Cf. p. 76, above.
[35] *Pierre Corneille,* p. 286.

Elle ne peut pas se maîtriser. Elle aime; tout ce qui contrarie cet amour n'existe plus pour cette femme passionée et tumultueuse. . . .[36]

Faguet indicated that the younger Horace's patriotism was a passion as uncontrollable as Camille's love for Curiace.[37] Faguet was, I believe, justified when he said that each character "a sa passion qu'il suit tout droit et qu'il n'y a nullement une partie de lui-même qui se batte contre l'autre." *Horace* represented "le choc l'une contre l'autre des deux plus grandes passions qui existent, l'amour et l'amour du pays." *Horace* does not portray the conflict between duty and love, but the conflict between two passions; love of country as personified by the younger Horace and love as personified by Camille. As Lemaître said, there is "un devoir indiscutable," one's duty to one's country which sets the action of the play in motion, but patriotism for the younger Horace is a passion, not a duty. Duty serves only to create the situation.

Although it is my intention to put aside the technique of the theater and, in particular, the three unities, it would

---

[36] Sarcey, *Quarante Ans de Théâtre* (Paris: Bibliothèque des Annales, 1900), I, 25.

[37] Lanson, on the other hand, maintained that Corneille does not want to portray passion as "une impulsion inconsciente": "Il ne la laisse agir que transposée en maxime réfléchie. C'est ce qu'on voit dans *Horace*: . . . Camille raisonne, Horace raisonne. Parce que Camille s'estime obligée de préférer son amour à toute chose, elle veut gâter la victoire de son frère, qui lui a tué son amant; sa malédiction sur Rome n'éclate point comme l'explosion involontaire d'une âme trop pleine: c'est une démarche calculée, à laquelle elle s'est mûrement excitée. Ce n'est pas une folle douleur, mais une *vendetta* froide. Et parce qu'Horace s'estime obligé de préférer à toute chose sa patrie, il ne tolère point la malédiction de sa soeur; il la tue par 'raison'; là non plus il n'y a pas une folie féroce, mais une froide justice." (*Op. cit.,* pp. 103-104.)

be almost impossible not to mention the unity of action in *Horace*. This feature of the play has been discussed by most critics since the seventeenth century. In his *Discours des Trois Unités*, Corneille defined the unity of action as the unity of peril:

> Je tiens donc, et je l'ai déjà dit, que l'unité d'action consiste . . . en l'unité de péril dans la tragédie, soit que son héros y succombe, soit qu'il en sorte.[38]

Most critics consider the murder of Camille the weakest point in the play because it is an event for which we have not been prepared. It is thought of as a means devised by Corneille to prolong the play because the younger Horace emerges from the first peril at the end of Act III. Act V is usually considered dull and useless. Corneille realized, perhaps more clearly than anyone else, that Camille's death weakens the unity of action.[39]

---

[38] *Op. cit.*, Vol. I.

[39] " . . . cette action, qui devient la principale de la pièce, est momentanée, et n'a point cette juste grandeur que lui demande Aristote et qui consiste en un commencement, un milieu et une fin. Elle surprend tout d'un coup; et toute la préparation que j'y ai donnée par la peinture de la vertu farouche d'Horace, et par la défense qu'il fait à sa soeur de regretter qui que ce soit, de lui ou de son amant, qui meure au combat, n'est point suffisante pour faire attendre un emportement si extraordinaire, et servir de commencement à cette action. . . . cette mort fait une action double, par le second péril où tombe Horace après être sorti du premier . . . où Horace revient triomphant sans aucun besoin de tuer sa soeur, ni même de parler à elle; et l'action serait insuffisamment terminée à sa victoire. Cette chute d'un péril en l'autre, sans nécessité, fait ici un effet d'autant plus mauvais, que d'un péril public, où il y va de tout l'Etat, il tombe en un péril particulier, où il n'y va que de sa vie, et pour dire encore plus, d'un péril illustre, où il ne peut succomber que glorieusement en un péril infâme, dont il ne peut sortir sans tâche." (*Op. cit., Examen d'Horace*, Vol. I.)

While Brunetière, Lemaître, Rigal, and Lanson criticized the play for the same reason, Faguet defended Corneille against himself and in so doing presented a rather unusual interpretation of the play. Corneille said that Camille's death exposed Horace to a second peril "qui n'est pas nécessairement amené par le premier." Faguet agreed, but asserted that the second peril was

> ... vraisemblablement amené par le premier. Horace, tout chaud encore de sa bataille et de sa victoire, éperdu d'orgueil patriotique et d'orgueil personnel, ne rencontre pas nécessairement sa soeur; mais il est très vraisemblable qu'il la rencontre puisqu'il rentre chez lui et peu s'en faut que ce ne soit nécessaire; le second péril était donc parfaitement contenu dans le premier et à le bien prendre il n'y a qu'une action.[40]

Although Corneille maintained that the younger Horace's order to Camille not to cry for either him or Curiace after the battle did not sufficiently prepare the spectator for her death, Faguet disagreed: Camille's death

> ... est le modèle même des coups de théâtre, ... un événement auquel on ne s'attendait pas et auquel on devait s'attendre et qu'on reconnaît qu'on aurait dû prevoir.[41]

Faguet's thesis may be tenable, but it is doubtful whether Horace's order to Camille in Act II is sufficient preparation for the spectator, who has probably forgotten it by Act V. It is also doubtful whether Camille, because of her state of mind in Act II, would give Horace's order serious consideration. It seems strange that Corneille, who was such an acute and penetrating critic of his own plays, did not defend *Horace* in a similar manner.

Most nineteenth-century critics considered the younger

---

[40] *En lisant Corneille,* p. 118.
[41] *Ibid.,* p. 119.

Horace and Camille the principal characters of the play
and called Act V useless because Camille was dead at the
end of Act IV and Horace had already survived one peri
at the end of Act II. Faguet argued that Act V was the
most important act and the one that gave unity to the play

> Je défendrai Corneille ici très volontiers contre lui-même en
> disant d'abord que si le meurtre de Camille n'est pas contenu
> nécessairement dans la victoire d'Horace, il y est contenu assez
> vraisemblablement : en disant surtout que pourvu qu'il y ait une
> unité, quelle qu'elle soit du reste, dans une oeuvre d'art, il suffit ;
> qu'il peut y avoir par exemple une unité morale, une unité de
> sentiment général, à la condition toutefois que cette unité soit
> personnifieé, soit incarnée dans un personnage de l'unité d'Horace :
> c'est Horace qui fait l'unité d'*Horace*. A qui le spectateur s'in-
> téresse, à quoi du moins il doit s'intéresser, c'est à l'âme du vieil
> Horace, c'est à cet homme patriote et père, patriote ardent et père
> tendre qui au service de sa patrie se voit privé en un jour de
> trois de ses enfants sur quatre, qui supplie qu'on conserve "pour
> elle" ce quatrième. Tant qu'on ne saura pas ce qui est arrivé en
> définitive à ce personnage, il y aura unité de péril et par consé-
> quent unité d'action ; en tout cas il y aura unité et cela suffit.
> C'est ici, quoi que je vienne de dire, plutôt unité d'intérêt
> morale qu'une unité d'intérêt de curiosité.[42]

> C'est lui qui est l'âme de la pièce. Voilà ce que le spectateur
> doit comprendre, sans quoi il ne comprendra pas bien la pièce
> elle-même. Or, Horace le père court-il plusieurs dangers ? Il n'en
> court qu'un, c'est que dans cette guerre, par ses coups et ses con-
> tre-coups, sa famille entière ne périsse, fils, fille et bru. Tant que
> lui reste une branche de son tronc, il n'est pas sorti de péril . . .
> Il y a donc péril contenu qui ne finit qu'à la dernière scène du
> cinquième acte, il y a donc unité de péril et donc unité d'action.[43]

Faguet's thesis is interesting but not completely justi-

---

[42] *Ibid.*, p. 73.
[43] *Ibid.*, p. 119.

fiable upon close examination of the character of the elder Horace. During Act I and most of Act II our attention is directed towards the younger Horace, Curiace, and Camille. The elder Horace first appears in Act II when he encourages Horace and Curiace to carry out their duty rather than listen to the entreaties of Camille and Sabine. In Act III the elder Horace, hearing the false report of his son's fleeing from the battle, says that he would have preferred to have his son die a glorious and honorable death serving his country than alive and dishonored. His only attempt to save the younger Horace is his appeal to the king in Act V:

> Rome aujourd'hui m'a vu père de quatre enfants;
> Trois en ce même jour sont morts pour sa querelle;
> Il m'en reste encore un, conservez-le pour elle.[44]

The elder Horace is motivated primarily by his patriotism and his sense of honor. To punish the younger Horace for his sister's murder would dishonor him, and more than anything else the elder Horace wishes to preserve his family's honor.

The suggestion is not intended that the elder Horace is cold and inhuman. Although Sarcey[45] and Lemaître[46] supported Faguet's contention that the elder Horace was "un tendre père" and "le personnage le plus humain" of the play, the elder Horace does nothing to save his sons at the beginning of the play, because he realizes that there is nothing to be done.

Faguet is the only critic mentioned in this chapter who maintained that the elder Horace was the principal char-

---

[44] V, 7.

[45] "Le vieil Horace, père si humain et si facile aux grands attendrissements." (*Op. cit.*, II, 19.)

[46] ". . . l'amour de la patrie s'adoucit chez le vieil Horace par l'âge et la paternité." (*Pierre Corneille*, p. 285.)

acter and the connecting link in the unity of the play.[47]
Faguet himself realized the shortcomings of his thesis:

> A mon avis le vieil Horace est le personnage principal de cette
> tragédie, c'est la vérité, mais Corneille ne l'a pas encore assez
> marqué. Certes il a presque prodigué le vieil Horace sur le théâtre
> et aux moments les plus décisifs. Il ne l'a pas montré encore assez.
> Il devait le faire assister à la mort de Camille puisque c'est lui
> qui est le lien dramaturgique entre l'épisode précédent et celui-ci,
> et puisque c'est sur lui, en même temps que sur son fils, que le
> premier péril passé, ce second péril retombe.[48]

The younger Horace and Camille are both motivated
by passion and neither one experiences a conflict between
duty and passion. The intrigue is in itself enough to shock
the spectator and at the same time arouse his curiosity. We
may admire the younger Horace's energy and determination; but do we admire his actions? *Horace* is the portrayal
of limitless energy motivated by a shocking passion.

Most of Corneille's plays that appear to be based on
the conflict between duty and passion cannot be classified
with *le Cid* and *Horace*.[49] If any of the other plays do in-
volve the fulfillment of a duty—and that is not always
true—it is a very special type of duty, it is one that is in-

---

[47] Lanson, on the other hand, said that the younger Horace and
Camille were the principal characters and that the unity of the play
". . . est rétablie par les caractères. . . . *Horace* semble constitué par
trois actions successives, un combat, un meurtre, un jugement: les
caractères du jeune Horace et de Camille resserreront cette matière
disjointe, et fourniront une liaison morale. Horace vainqueur, il faut
que Camille entre en action; cette victoire l'y force, et elle force son
frère au meurtre, dont il ne saurait ni être puni ni se repentir. Voilà
toute la tragédie unifiée par ces deux âmes." (*Op. cit.,* p. 128.)

[48] *En lisant Corneille,* p. 121.

[49] While I support Faguet's thesis that *Horace* illustrated the
shock of two opposing passions, rather than a conflict between duty
and passion, he realized that a very real duty set the play in motion.

vented or imagined by the hero. It will be recalled that late-nineteenth-century critics believed that the Cornelian hero used his will to overcome his feelings and thus demonstrated to himself and to others that he was the master of his destiny.[50] Faguet's contention that *Cinna* was a perfect example of the Cornelian hero's endeavor to dominate his sentiments[51] was supported by Lemaître:

> . . . on rencontre déjà dans *Cinna* ce qui caractérisera la plupart des tragédies postérieures à *Polyeucte*: l'effort de la volonté admiré pour lui-même et indépendamment du but.[52]

Lanson reinforced this interpretation, emphasizing that the Cornelian hero strove to convince himself that he was responsible for his destiny.[53]

Cinna was criticized during the eighteenth century because Cinna, the apparent hero, was considered cowardly and base.[54] This interpretation was generally maintained

---

[50] Cf. pp. 67-68, above.

[51] "Auguste est fatigué; il veut abdiquer; un de ses conseillers lui conseille de le faire, un autre . . . l'en dissuade. Il apprend ensuite que celui-là même qui l'a retenu sur le trône dirige une conspiration contre lui. Il s'indigne et en même temps s'exaspère. Il songe à quitter la vie, et il songe à punir et à venger. Il appelle à lui le chef des conjurés. Il l'accable de reproches sanglants sans savoir encore ce qu'il fera. Mais en humiliant et ravalant son rival, il s'aperçoit qu'il se venge. En satisfaisant ainsi partiellement son désir de vengeance, il s'en purge et il s'aperçoit qu'il s'en purge en effet et alors il est disposé au pardon. En considérant que le pardon est une grande victoire sur lui-même, il s'exalte dans cette idée de pardon; il tend toute sa volonté pour se vaincre, pour avoir le plaisir d'épuiser toute sa volonté et il pardonne. . . ." (*En lisant Corneille,* p. 123.)

[52] *Pierre Corneille,* p. 292.

[53] ". . . Auguste voit plus de grandeur à vaincre en soi la volonté de punir qu'à punir en effet. Il pardonne, quoi qu'il en doive advenir: il a mis son bonheur à ne dépendre que de soi en se rendant maître de soi." (*Op. cit.,* p. 113.)

[54] Cf. p. 41, above.

during the second half of the nineteenth century. *Cinna* was also criticized in the eighteenth century because of the shift of interest from Cinna to Auguste.[55] La Harpe was the first to maintain that the most interesting character in the play was Auguste,[56] and Janin, in complete accord, said that Auguste was not only the most interesting role in *Cinna*, but was the major one and the unifying element of the play.[57] Janin's interpretation of the role of Auguste as the portrayal of the evolution of a character was maintained throughout the latter half of the nineteenth century and concisely resumed by Faguet:

> Le même homme qui combattait, proscrivait, tuait pour arriver au pouvoir, *se combat et proscrit en lui le proscripteur et tue en lui le vindicatif* pour arriver au suprême pouvoir qui est la domination de soi-même. Or, c'est là précisément la véritable évolution de caractère. Une évolution de caractère n'est naturelle, n'est logique et n'est véritable que quand la faculté maîtresse qui constituait le caractère ancien, persistant, mais transformée et épurée par les circonstances et les épreuves, ou transformée et dégradée par les circonstances et les épreuves prend caractère nouveau.[58]

Besides reinforcing Janin's interpretation, Faguet undertook, as he did with *Horace*, to defend Corneille against the charge that the shift of interest from Cinna to Auguste weakened the play. In Act I our attention is directed to Cinna and Emilie, whereas in Act II, Auguste seems to be the major role. Auguste does not appear in Act III and our interest reverts to Cinna. Faguet defended Corneille: if the spectator

---

[55] *Ibid.*
[56] Cf. p. 42, above.
[57] Cf. p. 61, above.
[58] *En lisant Corneille,* p. 129.

... attache son intérêt à Cinna au premier acte il a un peu tort et que s'il l'attache à Cinna au second acte il a tort complète- ment et que l'auteur ne peut pas être tout à fait responsable des erreurs du public. Si le spectateur attache son intérêt à Cinna au premier acte il a déjà un peu tort, car si un conspirateur est tou- jours intéressant, un conspirateur par amour et par vanité ne devrait pas l'être. Or c'est absolument tel que Corneille nous pré- sente son Cinna. ... Si le spectateur continue de l'aimer au second acte il est encore moins dans le bon sens; car tout de suite Auguste y fait figure de très honnête homme et de personnage très sympathique et Cinna y joue un très vilain personnage. Quel est l'honnête homme dans le parterre qui peut être pour Cinna dès la *première* scène de l'acte II? Il n'y a donc pas, il ne doit pas y avoir déplacement d'intérêt, ou s'il y a, pour mettre les choses au mieux des intérêts de ceux que je contredis, déplacement d'intérêt il ne peut être qu'à la première scène de l'acte II et non pas plus loin. La faute, s'il y a faute, est donc très légère.[59]

No other critic of this period attempted to defend Cor- neille in this manner. Although Faguet's interpretation is not without foundation, it would appear to be based on pro- longed meditation and careful reading of the play rather than on a first, or even second, impression. Except for this one aspect of *Cinna* the period was essentially unanimous in its judgment of the play.

Seventeenth- and eighteenth-century interpretations of *Polyeucte* were concerned primarily with Pauline's love for Sévère and her duty towards Polyeucte. Whether Pauline would remain faithful to her husband or marry Sévère after Polyeucte's death was, for seventeenth- and eighteenth- century critics, the most interesting feature of the play.[60] Although Sainte-Beuve did not depreciate Pauline's conflict, he was the earliest critic to insist upon the importance of

[59] *Ibid.,* pp. 132-133.
[60] Cf. pp. 36, 43-44, above.

the religious theme: the martyrdom of Polyeucte and the effect of divine grace.[61]

Most critics in the second half of the nineteenth century, perhaps influenced by Sainte-Beuve, considered the religious theme the dominant feature of the play. Lemaître's contention that *Polyeucte* was a tableau of the early rise of Christianity as well as a portrayal of the effect of divine grace[62] was sustained by Rigal:

> . . . Corneille doit traduire de la façon la plus nette et la plus dramatique possible cette idée chrétienne de la grâce: c'est avec l'eau du baptême que Polyeucte recevra la force de proclamer sa foi devant les prêtres païens comme devant les bourreaux. Aucun auteur de mystères eût-il trouvé traduction plus saisissante, sans grossier réalisme, de l'acte divin qui est le point de départ de la tragédie?[63]

This attitude, maintained throughout the century, was reinforced by Faguet:

> Corneille a, faisant un drame chrétien, accepté et admis tout le christianisme comme matière, comme ressort et comme couleur. Il a introduit dans sa pièce la doctrine de la grâce, et l'a fait paraître, avec intention, dès les scènes d'exposition, comme il devait la faire éclater en son dénouement.[64]

> Toute une histoire de l'établissement du christianisme est dans ce drame. Par *Polyeucte* tout seul on peut apprendre que, pour s'établir, le christianisme a dû briser aux coeurs de ses disciples l'intérêt personnel, cela va de soi, et aussi les plus légitimes affections humaines, et l'idée de patrie, et la raison même.[65]

In spite of the importance they attached to this feature

---

[61] Cf. p. 62, above.

[62] Cf. *Impressions de Théâtre,* première série, p. 25.

[63] *Op. cit.,* p. 235.

[64] Emile Faguet, *Etudes Littéraires* (Paris: Lecène, Oudin, 1894), III, 16.

[65] *Propos de Théâtre,* première série, pp. 120-121.

of the play, Lemaître, Rigal, Sarcey, Faguet, and Lanson devoted more pages to Pauline's love for Polyeucte than to the religious significance of *Polyeucte*. Sarcey, while not denying the importance of the play's religious implications, considered Pauline the most interesting character. The one question the spectator asked himself was—

> Que va-t-elle faire? il n'y a pour une femme que deux issues à cette situation: il faut qu'elle en arrive à détester son mari, ou bien à l'adorer. De quel côté tournera-t-elle? C'est là qu'est le drame, drame intime, et mille fois plus intéressant pour nous que les tirades sur le christianisme: car c'est celui de toutes les femmes à un certain moment de leur vie. . . .[66]

It would seem that although late-nineteenth-century critics considered Polyeucte's martyrdom the most important aspect of the play, they found Pauline's conflict more interesting. They generally agreed, moreover, that Pauline's dilemma was closely related to the theme of martyrdom. Faguet resumed this idea: what might appear to be two distinct situations in *Polyeucte* were in reality only one:

> Dans l'un et dans l'autre point de vue, c'est toujours un des deux drames que la pièce contient que l'on admire aux dépens de l'autre, et il resterait encore cette imperfection qu'il y avait deux actions différentes dans *Polyeucte*. Y en a-t-il donc vraiment deux? Non, il n'y en a bien qu'une. Il y a deux situations, qui, influant l'une sur l'autre, forment une seule action marchant droit à son but unique. Le lien de ces deux situations et le ressort par où elles pèsent l'une sur l'autre, c'est Pauline. Ce que l'on n'a pas compris quand on ne s'attachait qu'aux "tendres sentiments" de Sévère et de Pauline, ou quand on ne voyait dans le drame que la grande figure de Polyeucte, c'est que Pauline aime Sévère au commencement du drame, et qu'elle aime Polyeucte à la fin. . . .[67]

---

[66] *Op. cit.,* III, 54.
[67] *Etudes Littéraires,* p. 26.

Seventeenth- and eighteenth-century critics generally agreed that Pauline did not love Polyeucte at the end of the play and that she remained faithful to him only out of her sense of duty.[68] Sainte-Beuve's contention that Pauline loved Sévère at the beginning of the play and Polyeucte at the end[69] was maintained during the second half of the nineteenth century by Lemaître,[70] Rigal,[71] Faguet,[72] and Lanson.[73]

While some critics said that her attachment to Polyeucte at the beginning of the play was based solely upon her sense of conjugal duty, others said that she had a real affection for Polyeucte.[74] Whichever may be true is a basically insignifi-

---

[68] Cf. p. 36, above.

[69] Cf. p. 65, above.

[70] "Voilà pourtant, disait-on au XVIIe siècle, une honnête femme qui n'aime pas son mari." C'est là une impression un peu trop superficielle. Relisez la pièce: vous verrez que Pauline finit par aimer Polyeucte . . ." (*Impressions de Théâtre,* première série, p. 301.)

[71] ". . . Pauline n'avait guère de l'estime pour Polyeucte, et elle avait pour Sévère de l'amour; peu à peu c'est à l'estime—à l'estime profonde—qu'elle se borne vis-à-vis de Sévère, et l'amour naît et s'accroît sans cesse en son âme pour Polyeucte." (*Op. cit.,* p. 243.)

[72] Cf. n. 67, above.

[73] *Op. cit.,* pp. 110-111.

[74] While Sainte-Beuve said that Pauline didn't love Polyeucte when she married him, other critics said that she had a true affection for him at the beginning of the play. Critics seemed undecided about this point, particularly Faguet, whose works presented different interpretations:

"Il y a Pauline, partagée entre son ancien amour pour Sévère et *ses devoirs d'abord,* son admiration ensuite pour Polyeucte." (*Etudes Littéraires,* p. 24.)

"Il y a Pauline, partagée entre son ancien amour pour Sévère et *son affection d'abord,* son admiration ensuite pour Polyeucte." (*Propos de Théâtre,* I, 116.)

". . . c'est que Pauline aime Sévère au commencement du drame, et qu'elle aime Polyeucte à la fin; c'est que du sentiment du *"devoir"*

cant point that is overshadowed by one more important: how and why does her love for Polyeucte develop?

Sainte-Beuve maintained that Pauline's love for Polyeucte was based upon reason and that it was the only type of love she was capable of.[75] Rigal agreed:

> . . . Pauline arrive à l'amour par le devoir et par la volonté. Le devoir! il n'est pas de mot qui revienne plus fréquemment à la bouche de Pauline, sinon peut-être ceux de raison et de gloire; c'est la raison qui lui a fait surmonter ses premiers sentiments en faveur de Sévère et accepter l'époux que son père lui a choisi; c'est la raison qui étouffe en elle la passion, prête à renaître à la vue de Sévère . . . et enfin c'est le sentiment de sa gloire qui la soutient quand elle lutte contre son père, quand elle lutte contre Polyeucte lui-même, quand elle refuse Sévère et le force à se sacrifier si complètement, si héroïquement. . . .[76]

Lemaître did not care for Sainte-Beuve's and Rigal's interpretation: Pauline's love was not directed by reason, but there was

> . . . quelque chose de très féminin dans la transformation des sentiments de Pauline. Elle se met à aimer son mari, non seulement parce qu'il est en danger et qu'il va mourir, mais aussi parce qu'il est fou et que, tout au fond, la sagesse de Sévère lui parait un peu plate auprès de cette folie. Elle aime son mari par devoir, soit; mais aussi par pitié, et surtout parce qu'elle ne le comprend pas et qu'elle subit l'attrait de l'inexpliqué et de l'inconnu. A partir du moment où Polyeucte lui dit: "Laissez-moi tran-

---

qui l'attache à Polyeucte au début . . ." (*Etudes Littéraires,* p. 26.)

"... c'est que Pauline aime encore Sévère et *aime déjà Polyeucte au commencement du drame,* . . . c'est que du sentiment du devoir et *d'un commencement d'amour qui l'attache* à Polyeucte au début . . ." (*Propos de Théâtre,* I, 118; italics supplied.)

[75] Cf. p. 65, above.

[76] *Op. cit.,* p. 257.

quille" et "Epousez Sévère après ma mort", soyez sûrs que l'âme de Pauline est tout entière à son mari, et elle est encore plus à lui après qu'elle l'a vu mourir. Le bon Corneille nous dit qu'elle a été subitement éclairée par la grâce. Non, non, c'est par amour qu'elle se fait chrétienne. Pauline, avec ses apparences de santé morale et de bel équilibre, serait donc la plus femme des femmes de Corneille, un être faible et généreux que l'extraordinaire attire, et qui est beaucoup plus conduit par son imagination et sa sensibilité que par sa raison; c'est-à-dire ce qu'il y a de plus contraire à l'idée que l'on se fait communément d'une héroïne cornélienne.[77]

Faguet's interpretation of Pauline's love was essentially the same as Lemaître's except that he attributtd her conversion to Christianity as an effect of divine grace and admiration for Polyeucte:

Pauline est généreuse et héroïque du fond de l'âme; mais elle est femme, c'est-à-dire un être chez lequel l'héroïsme est sentiment, non idée, et qui, quand Polyeucte se sacrifie, se sacrifie à une personne, non à une foi, ou du moins à cette foi, à cause de cette personne. L'instinct du devoir la détache de Sévère, l'attache à Polyeucte. Toutefois elle est païenne, et désapprouve le sacrilège de Polyeucte. Mais Polyeucte devient si grand qu'elle est comme enflammée de l'admiration qu'il lui inspire. L'affection l'entraîne sur les pas du martyr; la grâce fait le reste.[78]

Lanson presented a compromise between the ideas of Lemaître and Faguet, and of Rigal and Sainte-Beuve: that the acts of Corneille's characters were directed by reason—reason that evolved logically from their *idée fixe*.[79] He declared that Corneille's characters based their love on the idea of absolute perfection. The object loved represented

[77] *Impressions de Théâtre,* première série, p. 30.
[78] *Etudes Littéraires*, p. 18.
[79] Cf. p. 71, above.

perfection.[80] Pauline's love for Polyeucte was the result of both reason and sentiment:

Pauline a d'abord pour Polyeucte une affection paisible, raisonnable, d'estime pour l'honnête homme, de devoir pour le mari. L'inclination, comme elle le dit, va à Sévère . . . Mais à mesure que la pièce se développe, l'exaltation chrétienne de Polyeucte fait pâlir les vertus humaines de Sévère. Elle conçoit de combien ce mari qui, l'aimant, la possédant, renonce à elle, et sacrifie son bien réel à une idée, est plus grand que cet amant qui met en elle son bien souverain et toute sa raison d'agir. Sa générosité lui commande d'être avec celui qui se perd et qui perd tout, non avec celui qui profitera par cette perte. Aussi, tandis que sa volonté choisit le plus difficile, comme étant le plus sûr, son amour le lui rend facile, en se portant d'une perfection moindre vers une perfection plus haute: admiratrice tout à l'heure de la noblesse stoïcienne de Sévère, elle est transportée maintenant par la saintêté chrétienne de Polyeucte. L'amour de Sévère, maintenant, c'est le passé: le présent, c'est qu'elle "adore" son mari. Elle ne peut donc s'abstenir de tendre à s'unir avec lui: et c'est ainsi qu'il l'emporte après lui jusqu'à Dieu; sa conversion est la preuve qu'elle a une claire notion de la source d'où jaillissait l'héroïsme de Polyeucte. Voilà une femme qui aime deux hommes, déplace sa préférence de l'un à l'autre, et aboutit enfin à se reposer en Dieu: c'est toute une vie morale qui tient dans une crise, et toute une âme, sentiment, raison, volonté, qui se renouvelle en souffrant.[81]

---

[80] Although Lanson maintained that the exercise of will in Cornelian tragedy was directed by reason, he indicated that the Cornelian hero often confused will and passion because ". . . la passion nous conduit à ce qu'on sent être le bien par une révélation intuitive; la volonté nous mène à ce qu'on sait être le bien par un examen réfléchi: Ainsi par la vérité de la connaissance, ou même lorsque la raison cède à l'erreur du sentiment, la passion et la volonté se confondent, et comme se fondent dans un acte unique." (*Op. cit.*, p. 107.)

[81] *Ibid.*, p. 111.

Nineteenth-century interpretations of *Polyeucte* presented striking contrasts to the generally accepted interpretations of the seventeeth and eighteenth centuries. Pauline was no longer called "une honnête femme qui n'aime pas son mari," and the earlier objections to *Polyeucte*'s religious implications were greatly modified. As a matter of fact, late-nineteenth-century critics considered the religious theme the essential motivating principle of the play.

CHAPTER FOUR

The Legend Further Modified
in the Twentieth Century

THE works of the twentieth-century critics who will be discussed in this chapter illustrate three important trends in their approach to Cornelian criticism. Just as the late nineteenth century reacted against the earlier interpretation of Cornelian tragedy as the portrayal of conflict between duty and passion, so the twentieth century condemns the trend of late-nineteenth-century critics to present Cornelian tragedy as an example of the glorification of will. Although many eighteenth- and nineteenth-century critics suggested, in passing, that Corneille's plays often depicted events that actually occurred during the poet's life as well as the literary and philosophical ideas of his era, no literary critic before the twentieth century seriously developed this aspect of Cornelian tragedy. The third trend is the concern for Corneille's comedies and for those tragedies written after *Rodogune*. Nineteenth-century critics generally discussed at length *le Cid*, *Horace*, *Cinna*, and *Polyeucte*, and referred to Corneille's comedies and later tragedies only when they found it necessary to substantiate more fully some aspect of his theater. Twentieth-century critics, on the other hand, tend to emphasize the importance of his comedies and later tragedies. These three trends, which are prevalent throughout most twentieth-century criticism of Cornelian tragedy, are intimately related. The importance assigned to Corneille's comedies and later tragedies, together with the attempt to show that his plays were influenced by the literary, political, and philosophical ideas of the seventeenth century, is a reaction against the systematization of Cornelian tragedy by late-nineteenth-century critics.

While most twentieth-century critics do not deny that the theme of will is a dominant element of Cornelian tragedy, they condemn the late nineteenth-century interpretation that attributed to Corneille the creation of the superhuman hero. Brasillach directly criticizes it:

> Ce sont les professeurs en effet qui ont contribué à accuser chez Corneille cet aspect volontaire, qui existe sans doute, mais dont l'importance ne nous paraît au premier abord aussi grande que l'importance de la tentation romanesque.[1]

Adam reinforces Brasillach's accusation: in *Horace*, Corneille does not follow any system, but—

> Il réalise simplement un type d'homme héroïque qu'il porte en son esprit, et qui y est né, non pas de vues théoriques, mais d'une observation profonde de la réalité contemporaine. Il n'oppose pas les uns aux autres des concepts abstraits: raison et passion, devoir et crime, volonté et sentiment. Il voit.[2]

Adam pursues this view in his discussion of *Polyeucte*:

> Prenons garde pourtant de ne pas attribuer à Corneille une psychologie de l'héroïsme qui ne lui est nullement propre. Aux yeux de bien des commentateurs, c'est Corneille qui a créé ce type magnifique du héros qui domine à ce point le tulmulte de ses sentiments qu'il lui est possible d'aimer ou de n'aimer pas, et qui laisse aux lois du devoir une puissance absolue sur son coeur. S'il est pourtant un point où le rôle de Corneille ne fut pas crèateur et où il se borne à donner une expression magnifique à un lieu commun de la littérature du temps, c'est celui-là.[3]

Brasillach's and Adam's emphasis on the influence of

---

[1] Robert Brasillach, *Corneille* (Paris: Arthème Fayard, 1938), p. 142.

[2] Antoine Adam, *Histoire de la Littérature Française au XVIIe Siècle* (5 vols.; Paris: Domat, 1949-1956), I, 527.

[3] *Ibid.,* p. 541.

seventeenth-century literary themes in Cornelian tragedy is not a new idea, but rather a confirmation of twentieth-century endeavor to refute the earlier inclination to attribute to Corneille the invention of a superhuman hero. Dorchain's *Corneille* is a literary criticism of Corneille's theater, a biography of the dramatist, and a history of the period. It is one of the earliest indications of the new century's proclivity to explain Corneille's theater through the author's life and the era in which he lived. Although Dorchain offers many examples of how the events of the period and the general seventeenth-century literary atmosphere influenced the creation of Corneille's characters, his underlying theme is that Corneille invented his heroes to compensate himself for his own failures.[4] The creation of a hero capable of dominating his feelings is Corneille's way of fulfilling his unattained dreams and ideals:

> Corneille lui-même . . . en imagination, se plaît à ressusciter, à poursuivre, à atteindre une vieille chimère . . . qui est un des besoins profonds de sa nature, et par lesquels il compense ou répare, en rêve, les disgrâces que, dans le réel, lui ont infligées des circonstances, des rencontres, des conditions inégales à son génie.[5]

Although Rivaille's *Les Débuts de P. Corneille* is concerned only with Corneille's first six comedies and shares Dorchain's tendency to explain Corneille's theater apart from *Le Cid, Horace, Cinna,* and *Polyeucte,* Rivaille suggests that the dominant elements of Cornelian tragedy have their origin in his early comedies. Whereas Dorchain studies the effect of contemporary events and of the dramatist's life

---

[4] Cf. Auguste Dorchain, *Pierre Corneille* (Paris: Garnier, 1918). Dorchain maintained that *le Cid* was the result of Corneille's unhappy love affair with Catherine Hue (cf. p. 146); that Emilie was the typical heroine of *La Fronde* (cf. p. 205); that *Polyeucte,* written shortly after Corneille's marriage to Marie de Lampérière, was also a reflection of his personal life (cf. pp. 205-206).

[5] *Ibid.,* p. 450.

on his theater, Rivaille points out the influence of contemporary literary, philosophical, and religious ideas on the creation of the Cornelian hero. He contends that there are two themes prevalent in Corneille's comedies, which, although contradictory in nature, nonetheless exist in most of his plays. One of these is Corneille's preoccupation with *l'amour précieux*:

> Corneille montre un goût évident pour la vie mondaine et la recherche des plaisirs que l'on y admet. Comme chez la plupart des jeunes, une certaine conception de l'amour,—qui est très loin d'être l'obsession ou le culte, et qui tient largement de ce que l'on nommait jadis la galanterie,—y occupe une primauté incontestée. De là le goût d'une vie sentimentale plutôt qu'amoureuse, faite de plus d'idées que d'actes, avide surtout de sentiments, doux ou exaltés, et aussi du plaisir de briller et conquérir par le déploiement de toutes les ressources de l'ingéniosité et de l'esprit.[6]

The other tendency is the hero's search for truth, which

> ... se traduit par un effort continuel pour atteindre à une connaissance exacte ... Cette recherche de la vérité n'est pas uniquement l'oeuvre de son intelligence. Elle demande constamment le concours de sa volonté, soit que celle-ci sanctionne les propositions de l'intelligence, soit qu'elle la soutienne dans le labeur de sa poursuite ou l'excite à sa tâche. Vouloir, autant que savoir, est indispensable au bon exercice de l'esprit humain. Tous les personnages de Corneille sont conscients de l'effort volontaire que demande leur vie morale; presque tous s'appliquent à développer la puissance de leur volonté; ... Ils sentent que leur libre-arbitre est la condition la plus nécessaire à leur vie morale: que servirait d'être capable de découvrir la vérité, de disposer d'une force d'âme invincible. ...[7]

---

[6] Louis Rivaille, *Les Débuts de P. Corneille* (Paris: Boivin, 1936), p. 744.

[7] *Ibid.,* p. 459.

By maintaining that the predominant theme in Corneille's theater is how man's will, directed by reason, subjugates feelings, Rivaille reinforces the interpretation of Cornelian tragedy generally accepted in the second half of the nineteenth century.[8] But unlike his predecessors, Rivaille does not attribute to Corneille the invention of *le héros de la volonté;*[9] he insists that Corneille adopted a conception of life professed by the Jesuits:

> La manière dont Corneille a fait penser et parler ses personnages suffirait, seule, à montrer que sa conception du rôle joué par la raison et la volonté dans l'activité de l'âme humaine ne diffère pas de celle que professaient les scolastiques et les Jésuits, ses maîtres.[10]

In his *Plaisir à Corneille*, Schlumberger, like Rivaille and Dorchain, contends that Corneille's plays were influenced by events of the period, contain many of the themes of the romanesque literature of the era, and depict heroes capable of exercising their will to dominate their passions; but he does not seriously develop any of these themes.[11] His

---

[8] Cf. pp. 68-72, above.

[9] "Il est possible de dire que cette pensée dont Corneille alimentait toutes ses premières oeuvres, est personnelle, si l'on entend par là qu'il l'avait adoptée, qu'il l'avait faite sienne, mais non qu'il l'avait inventée ou créé." (*Op. cit.,* p. 555.)

[10] *Ibid.,* p. 500.

[11] It will be recalled that the aim of Rivaille's work is to show that the Cornelian hero has his origins in Corneille's comedies. Schlumberger declares that Corneille was essentially a writer of tragi-comedies and that he wrote *le Cid, Horace, Cinna,* and *Polyeucte* only to please a public who wished to see tragedies: "Le retour d'un certain ton spirituel et la fréquence des disparates m'induisaient à douter que l'axe central du gênie cornélien fût à chercher dans ses quelques tragédies véritables. Je soutins que par nature et par goût profond Corneille était un auteur de tragi-comédies. . . ." (Jean Schlumberger, *Plaisir à Corneille* [Paris: Gallimard, 1936], p. 15.)

work is neither a biography of Corneille nor a literary criticism in the strict meaning of the term. Schlumberger maintains that Corneille has always been disadvantaged by the innumerable comparisons between him and Racine, whose verse has usually been considered more beautiful and melodious. His major concern in examining Corneille's plays is to indicate the beauty of Cornelian verse.[12]

Brasillach treats all of Corneille's plays and, like Dorchain, tries to re-create the era in which Corneille lived in order to show the influence on his theater of events and ideas. Like Rivaille, he declares that the theme of will in both Cornelian tragedy and comedy was due to the influence of the Jesuits who directed Corneille's early education. Although he directly assails late-nineteenth-century critics for attributing to Corneille the creation of *le héros de la volonté*,[13] he says that will is a principal theme in Corneille's plays, second only to the *précieux* and romanesque elements:

> Il suffirait de reprendre les uns après les autres les thèmes des oeuvres de Corneille, tout au long de sa vie, pour découvrir, tout d'abord, beaucoup plus que le devoir ou la volonté, ce goût invincible du romanesque.[14]

Brasillach insists that Corneille's first tragedy, *Médée*, illustrates the romanesque tendency of his theater,[15] and

---

[12] ". . . la première chose est de retrouver un contact réel avec la poésie cornélienne, avec des rythmes, des cadences, des mots magiques. . . . Il s'agit donc de partir en exploration, sans idée préconçue, et de ramasser tout ce qui peut nous plaire." (*Ibid.*)

[13] Cf. p. 96.

[14] *Op. cit.*, p. 89.

[15] "C'est le goût du romanesque et de l'extravagant, n'en doutons pas, qui le pousse pourtant, lorsqu'enfin il veut écrire une tragédie régulière, à traduire du latin de Sénèque sa *Médée,* qui est une composition bien pompeuse." (*Ibid.*)

that his last work, *Suréna*, is also romanesque.[16] The Cornelian interpretation of reason, honor, love, and the struggle between duty and passion were all typical elements of the *précieux* novels of the period and Corneille did not create new ideas, but translated, in his own manner, those of *l'Astrée* and *la Clélie*:

> Et Pierre Corneille enfermait dans sa mémoire inconsciente tant de retenue et tant de hardiesse, comme il y avait enfermé la subtilité, la casuistique amoureuse, le goût du sacrifice, l'obéissance à l'amour parfait, et les innombrables démons charmants, rigoureux et fades, apprivoisés par Honoré d'Urfé, qu'il abriterait désormais, toute sa vie durant, dans son oeuvre. . . .[17]

Bénichou reinforces the propositions outlined by Dorchain, Rivaille, Schlumberger, and Brasillach: Corneille did not invent new ideas, but represented the ideas of his era. Bénichou contends that the political discussions in the plays echoed the ideas of the century[18] and that the Cornelian hero's attitude toward love, honor, and duty reflected the opinions of the nobility of the period:

> La création des valeurs héroïques va de pair, dans le milieu noble, avec une élaboration très particulière de l'instinct amoureux. C'est un penchant général de l'esprit chevaleresque que de faire de l'amour un stimulant à la grandeur. La conquête amoureuse reproduisait en effet avec ses compétitions, ses difficultés et sa gloire, la conquête militaire, et pouvait exiger les mêmes vertus. . . . L'amour est alors la récompense directe de la

---

[16] "Il réalise enfin ce qu'il espérait peut-être depuis sa lointaine jeunesse et la lecture enivrante de *l'Astrée*, une oeuvre entièrement et purement romanesque." (*Ibid.*, p. 349.)

[17] *Ibid.*, p. 65.

[18] "Corneille n'est pas théoricien de la politique. Mais ses personnages augmentent souvent, intercalent dans le drame l'écho des discussions politiques de son temps." (Paul Bénichou, *Morales du Grand Siècle* [Paris: 1940], p. 72.)

force et de la vaillance. Mais la conquête amoureuse préfère ordi-
nairement emprunter d'autres voies; un triomphe de pure force
sur la femme . . . ne flatterait guère des amateurs de prouesses
rares, et choquerait l'orgueil même . . . D'où le remplacement du
combat primitif par une lutte symbolique dans laquelle la femme
exige, pour céder à l'homme, qu'il se couvre de gloire au dehors.
Les exemples dans lesquels l'homme doit rechercher les grandeurs
pour obtenir de celle qu'il aime le consentement désiré abondent
dans Corneille.[19]

Nadal's *Le Sentiment de l'Amour dans l'Oeuvre de
Pierre Corneille* is primarily an analysis of *l'amour chevaleresque* in the Cornelian theater and reaffirms the modern
trend to minimize the importance of the theme of will in
Corneille's plays.[20] Nadal asserts, as do Schlumberger and
Brasillach, that the Cornelian theater is essentially romanesque[21] and that the ideals that govern all the heroic values
represented in the plays are identical to those upon which
the concept of *l'amour chevaleresque* is founded.[22] He supports Bénichou's proposition that *l'amant chevaleresque*

---

[19] *Ibid.*, p. 33.

[20] ". . . il nous a semblé difficile qu'on pût admettre le bien fondé
de l'analyse qui fait de la raison et de la volonté les principes de la
psychologie cornélienne et ramène celle-ci à l'idée de connaissance.
De même nous avons dénoncé la théorie de l'amour raisonnable, fondé
sur l'estime, et s'élevant par la connaissance des mérites jusqu'à l'idée
de la perfection ainsi que l'identité entrevue entre le 'héros cornélien'
et 'le généreux' selon Descartes, ou enfin la tentation de ramener
l'esthique cornélienne à la morale commune et plus arbitrairement à
la religion chrétienne." (Octave Nadal, *Le Sentiment de l'Amour
dans l'Oeuvre de Pierre Corneille* [Paris: Gallimard, 1948], p. 323.)

[21] "En réalité, dans ce théâtre, deux attitudes s'affrontent sans
cesse; elles peuvent se reduire au romanesque et au réalisme . . . Bref
la tendance romanesque met en constant péril la tendance raisonnable."
(*Ibid.*, p. 268.)

[22] ". . . la notion d'héroïsme cornélien est intimement parente de
celle d'amour héroïque." (*Ibid.*)

can win his loved one only "s'il se couvre de gloire," and says that the idea of *gloire* was the motivating element of the Cornelian theater:

> Toutes les lumières et toute la volonté du héros cornélien ne vont en fait qu'à reconnaître et à suivre les exigences de la Gloire. La générosité cornélienne est cette manière d'être du héros qui prend souci de ne pas se démentir aux yeux du monde et aux siens.[23]

> . . . l'idée de gloire nous a paru dominer la psychologie du théâtre cornélien et même donner son sens à l'oeuvre tout entière.[24]

Whereas Rivaille attributes the theme of will to the religious and philosophical ideas of the period, Nadal reinforces Schlumberger's and Brasillach's thesis: this was a romanesque idea founded upon the *chevaleresque* conception of *la gloire*.

It has been mentioned that Adam supports the modern trend to explain the role of will in Corneille's theater by declaring that Corneille did not invent new themes, but appropriated those of his era.[25] Among many examples[26] the

---

[23] *Ibid.*, p. 274.

[24] *Ibid.*, p. 322.

[25] Cf. pp. 96-97, above.

[26] Adam, like Brasillach, stresses the importance of the romanesque elements of Corneille's theater. Besides declaring that *le Cid* is a romanesque play (cf. Adam, *op. cit.*, Vol. 1, pp. 511-512), Adam also maintains that *La Mort de Pompée* is essentially romanesque: ". . . ces héros galants, ces héroïnes altières, Corneille les trouvait dans la littérature romanesque de son temps. La Calprenède, en 1642, commençait de publier son roman de *Cassandre*, vaste épopée où l'on trouverait sans peine, quantité de héros aussi intrépides et aussi amoureux que César, quantité d'héroïnes aussi fières que Cléopâtre. *La Mort de Pompée*, tragédie de forme classique et de sujet antique, est en réalité, par la psychologie de ses principaux personnages, une oeuvre romanesque." (*Op. cit.*, 11, 366.)

following most succinctly sums up Adam's thesis:

> Ce n'est pas Corneille, c'est toute sa génération qui a mis cette confiance sans limite dans la libre volonté de l'homme, dans son pouvoir sur les tumultes de la passion, dans sa victoire finale sur les désordres du sentiment.[27]

Herland's *Corneille* follows the general tendency of twentieth-century critics to present a literary criticism of all of Corneille's plays together with a biography of the dramatist and a history of the period. Whereas Rivaille, Schlumberger, Brasillach, and Adam indicate the influence of contemporary literary, social, and religious ideas on Corneille's theater, Herland minimizes these influences:

> Nous refusons pour notre part ce Corneille réduit aux fonctions d'un poste-relai. Nous refusons de reconnaître dans ses héros le type de héros qui se fabriquait en série dans la littérature du temps; à des degrés différents (car les oeuvres d'un grand écrivain n'ont pas toutes une égale sincérité), tous cependent se distinguent par une qualité d'âme qui n'est qu'à eux; leur grandeur est d'un autre ordre,—à la fois plus haute et plus vraie. Sans doute Corneille fut tributaire de son siècle, mais il lui rendit son bien méconnaissable.[28]

His thesis contains a major contradiction. He clearly states that an author's life is separate from his theater;[29] yet he tries to explain the Cornelian hero as a reflection of Corneille's personality and failures:

> Corneille s'est donné très tôt de la vie une vue triste et désenchantée. . . . Ce n'est pas seulement en effet dans les pièces de sa vieillesse que percent cette mélancolique acceptation du *sic transit*

[27] *Ibid.*, I, 542.

[28] Louis Herland, *Corneille* (Paris: Editions du Seuil, 1954), p. 81.

[29] "Sa vie fut une chose, son théâtre en est une autre." (*Ibid.*, p. 58.)

gloria mundi et cette sorte d'amertume sereine qui donne à *Tite
et Bérénice*, à *Pulchérie*, à *Suréna* une résonnance si profon-
dément humaine . . . En fait, passé *Le Cid*, on ne retrouve jamais
plus chez Corneille la franche gaîté de ses premières pièces, ni
cet accent triomphal et ce chant de confiance juvénile en la vie
qui avaient fait applaudir son Rodrigue.[30]

Herland maintains that Cornelian tragedy is the tragedy of
despair and failure,[31] and that the creation of the Cornelian
hero was influenced by defeats that Corneille had experienced in his personal and professional life. In this respect
Herland reinforces Dorchain's thesis, that Corneille's own
life influenced his work rather than the ideas of the century.

The critics who hold that Corneille incorporated the
generally accepted ideas of his time into his work would
seem to imply that Corneille's genius was not in creating
new themes, but rather in giving a more harmonious expression to existing ideals. To Herland, on the other hand, Corneille's theater does not necessarily express the ideals of the
period. Herland says that Cornelian tragedy is both epic
and realistic, and that Corneille's originality is his profound
observation of reality:

> . . . Corneille, créateur de héros, fut et demeure notre grand
> poète *épique* (exotisme et couleur locale écartés) : *épique*, parce
> que son imagination prodigieuse fait surgir de la fable ou de
> l'histoire, pour les dresser vivantes devant nous, de grandes figures

---

[30] *Ibid.*, pp. 88-89.

[31] "Disons d'une manière plus générale que le tragique cornélien
est toujours tragique de la déchéance (car cela peut arriver même à
des jeunes) ou de l'inégalité de valeur entre les hommes: tragique,
chez les meilleurs, de se sentir supérieurs à ceux qu'ils aiment; tragique,
chez les médiocres, de se sentir condamnés à être éternellement in-
férieurs à ces privilégiés, à ces enfants des dieux qui ne se sont donné
que la peine de naître pour se trouver nantis de tous les dons du ciel,
force, intelligence et magnanimité." (*Ibid.*, p. 92.)

étranges ou prestigieuses . . . Mais alors que Flaubert fit alterner les oeuvres de style épique et les oeuvres de style réaliste, Corneille au contraire mêle partout les deux tons et s'abandonne simultanément aux deux tendances de son génie: ces êtres supérieurs, ces créatures merveilleuses ou maléfiques, il les présente engagés dans des conflicts de famille ou des intrigues de palais dignes les uns de Balzac, les autres de Saint-Simon ou de Stendhal. . . . Nous avons le droit d'affirmer que très souvent, derrière les grands personnages dont l'histoire lui fournissait les noms, il eut en vue d'humbles drames de la société bourgeoise à laquelle il appartenait.[32]

Although the twentieth-century critics discussed here have reacted against the tendency of their immediate predecessors to stress the role of will in Cornelian tragedy, neither Dorchain, Rivaille, Bénichou, Adam, Nadal, nor Herland denies that this is a principal element of Corneille's theater. Although Schlumberger and Brasillach emphasize the romanesque aspect of Corneille's plays, they maintain that the theme of will is to be found or explained in the religious and romanesque sources of the period. The innovation of these modern critics is that they attribute to Corneille the dramatization of the common literary, social, and religious ideas of the seventeenth century rather than the creation of new themes. It cannot be denied that this recent trend to analyze all of Corneille's plays and to indicate the similarities between his theater and the period in which he lived is a valuable aid to a better understanding of the dramatist and, in a more general way, of the many complex and contradictory ideas of the seventeenth century.

In spite of the fact that most twentieth-century critics

---

[32] *Ibid.*, p. 91. Contrary to Herland, Giraudoux said that Corneille depicted extraordinary incidents. Cf. Giraudoux, "Racine," *La Nouvelle Revue Française*, CLXXXXV (1929), 744-746.

condemn systematization of the Cornelian hero, they generally support the interpretations of late-nineteenth-century critics. Critics in the second half of the nineteenth century maintained that the Cornelian hero was conscious of his actions, assumed full responsibility for the results, and believed that his fate was controlled by his own deliberate decisions.[33] Mornet's interpretation of the Cornelian hero is essentially the same as that of his immediate predecessors:

La tragédie cornélienne ne mettra pas en scène des volontés aveugles, mais des volontés réfléchies. Le héros de Corneille ressemble encore à celui de Descartes en ce sens qu'il a des idées claires et distinctes. . . . Corneille a su peindre des âmes où l'héroïsme n'est plus seulement une énergie impertubable, mais où il se mêle de souffrance, de trouble, où il est humain . . . c'est cette vérité humaine qui fait le pathétique cornélien. . . . C'est un arrachement cruel et héroïque où la décision généreuse élève l'homme au-dessus de lui-même.

Enfin, c'est un effort toujours lucide. Dans les meilleures pièces cornéliennes, le héros sait les difficultés de la lutte et conçoit les raisons de son effort. Il n'est pas seulement entraîné par un instinct généreux, par le besoin d'être grand. Il connaît les conditions et le prix de cette grandeur.[34]

Adam supports Mornet's contention by declaring that Corneille's characters represent—

Une volonté tendue à l'extrême. Un besoin d'absolue liberté. Quelque chose de stoïcien, dirait-on. Mais le stoïcisme est aussi une doctrine d'acceptation. Le héros cornélien n'accepte pas.[35]

Besides asserting that Corneille's plays represent the ideas of the period,[36] Adam declares that Corneille was a pro-

[33] Cf. pp. 67-68, above.
[34] Daniel Mornet, *Histoire Générale de la Littérature Française* (Paris: Larousse, n.d.), pp. 73-74.
[35] *Op. cit.*, I, 501.
[36] Cf. p. 96, above.

found observer of reality, and that his plays depict man's (especially the young man's) need to affirm his belief in his absolute liberty:

> Chose notable, sa vision s'attarde, avec une préférence certaine, sur la jeunesse. Rodrigue n'a guère que vingt ans et le jeune Horace n'en a guère davantage. Tout le sens des drames où ils sont mêlés s'affaiblit si on les imagine plus âgés. Qu'ils aient seulement trente ans, et Rodrigue tombe dans la sentimentalité romantique, et Horace n'est plus qu'une brute. Mais s'ils n'ont que vingt ans, tout ce qui étonne chez eux, tout ce qui nous paraît le résultat d'une vue systématique et forcée, se révèle normal, vrai, admirablement observé. Il appartenait à la jeunesse de se donner ainsi sans réserve ni partage à un haut idéal, d'y mettre une intransigeance que les sceptiques traitent de fanatisme, et qui traduit au contraire sa pureté.[37]

While Adam and Mornet fundamentally support the late-nineteenth-century interpretation of the Cornelian hero as the architect of his own destiny, Herland would have us believe that the Cornelian theater represents the tragedy of old age, despair, and failure:

> Horace a découvert les lendemains sinistres de la gloire, et Auguste, revenu de toutes les grandeurs de ce monde, prépare la voie à *Polyeucte*, suprême leçon de détachement et recours à l'autre vie comme à l'unique espérance. Et tous les autres, désormais, ou bien chercheront dans la gloire une raison désespérée de vivre, ou bien au contraire, indifférents à la gloire, ne penseront qu'à sauver leur part d'un bonheur fragile et périssable, tandis que les adolescents au coeur pur, à la première découverte qu'ils feront de la laideur de la vie, ne demanderont qu'à mourir, ayant d'un coup mesuré la néant de toutes choses.[38]

---

[37] *Op. cit.*, I, 527.
[38] *Op. cit.*, p. 89.

Contrary to Adam,[39] Herland declares not only that Cornelian tragedy depicts old age, despair, and failure, but that the Cornelian hero is generally confronted with a duty over which he has little control:

> Corneille . . . c'est le tragique de la condition de l'homme, que nous ne puissions jamais accomplir notre devoir sans faire souffrir quelqu'un, que toujours par quelque côté la justice soit contraire à la charité, qu'enfin le mal soient toujours intimement mêlés. Fatalité que seules les âmes les plus hautes et les plus délicates sont capables de ressentir douloureusement.[40]

His interpretation, which depicts the Cornelian hero chained by an uncontrollable fatality, is contrary to the generally accepted explanations of late-nineteenth-century and twentieth-century critics. It has been indicated that of all Corneille's tragedies, it is only in *le Cid* and *Horace* that the characters are confronted with a duty that they do not imagine and over which they have no control.[41] In most of Corneille's plays whatever duty is involved is usually invented by the principal character primarily so that he can prove to himself and to others that man makes his own decisions and is thus the master of his destiny. Herland does not accept this view, which depicts man as the apostle of liberty; although he agrees that the Cornelian theater is a theater of will, he sees it as a theater

> . . . de la volonté impuissante ou déchirée: car Corneille et ses personnages savent que l'homme est responsable de ses actes. . . . toujours ils s'efforcent de voir clair dans leur âme et de retrouver

---

[39] "L'héroïsme d'Horace, c'est l'héroïsme de la jeunesse, et Corneille, lorsqu'il écrit sa tragédie, n'est pas un esprit systématique qui construit et exploite une formule, mais un poète, épris de la beauté des âmes jeunes, des générosités intactes, des ardeurs qui ne calculent pas." (*Op. cit.*, I, 527.)

[40] *Op. cit.*, p. 98.

[41] Cf. pp. 59, 61, above.

la paix intérieure: . . . Incapables, sans un secours exceptionnel de la grâce, de parvenir à cette paix, ils savent du moins qu'ils ont toujours assez de liberté pour accomplir leur devoir. Pauvre liberté, qui sauve tout juste l'honneur! . . . Les meilleures tragédies de Corneille sont faites de ces combats douloureux pour une liberté dérisoire: l'homme y apparaît, non pas certes comme le vil esclave des passions, mais comme un homme libre enchaîné.[42]

Herland's thesis may be applicable to le Cid and Horace, but not to Corneille's other tragedies where the duty, if there is one, is created by the characters.

Some modern critics stress a feature of the Cornelian theater that their predecessors mentioned only in passing. Late-nineteenth-century critics directed attention to Corneille's penchant for brutal scenes and passions, but asserted that most of his characters (except for Médée and the Cléopâtre of Rodogune) were motivated by noble sentiments. Corneille's taste for brutality is considered by Schlumberger, Brasillach, and Adam a predominant trait of his theater.[43] Brasillach, commenting on Giraudoux's statement that almost all of Racine's tragedies are "tragédies de l'inceste et de la cohabitation,"[44] declares that "les tragédies de la haine familiale, c'est peut-être Corneille qui les a décrités."[45] He says that Corneille's plays present a tableau of cruel and inhuman parents:

Dès sa jeunesse, Corneille avait été attiré par la fable de Médée qui tue ses enfants: . . . Par la suite, que de Médées, que de massacres d'innocents dans son théâtre: depuis Don Diègue et le vieil Horace qui envoient leurs fils à la mort, depuis Félix, Valens, Prusias et Rodogune, et Marcelle, quelle effrayante galerie de pères criminels, de mères criminelles, quelle anticipation

[42] Op. cit., p. 99.
[43] Cf. Schlumberger, op. cit., pp. 46-48.
[44] Giraudoux, op. cit., p. 949.
[45] Op. cit., p. 212.

forcenée sur les pires imaginations de *Genitrix*! Les plus affreux
de ces monstres éclairent d'un jour singulier les plus modérés
d'entre eux, et c'est pourquoi sans doute les lois prudentes de
l'enseignement nous écartent de leur contact. Mais ils sont là, et
il n'est pas très difficile de pénétrer jusqu'à la porte de la mé-
nagerie.[46]

Adam also notes Corneille's penchant for brutality:

La première tragédie de Corneille mettra sur la scène l'horrible légende de Médée. La scène finale de *Rodogune* est connue,
et *Théodore* prouve qu'à cinquante ans il n'avait pas perdu le
sens des situations audacieuses et brutales.[47]

    Corneille, dès qu'il quitte la comédie de moeurs, aime les
situations fortes, les actions brutales. Il a un certain goût de
l'horrible. . . . Il n'y renoncera qu'à son corps défendant.[48]

While Brasillach and Adam underline the brutal aspect
of Corneille's theater, Péguy asserts that Corneille is incapable of creating a cruel or inhuman character.[49] Péguy,
a fervent admirer of Corneille and a predominantly Cath-
olic poet, considers *Polyeucte* not only the most beautiful
tragedy ever written, but the final expression of Corneille's

[46] *Ibid.*, p. 216.
[47] *Op. cit.*, I, 486.
[48] *Ibid.*, p. 501.
[49] "Corneille ne travaille jamais que dans le domaine de la grâce
. . . Racine ne travaille jamais que dans le domaine de la disgrâce.
Corneille n'opère jamais que dans le royaume du salut, Racine n'opère
jamais que dans le royaume de la perdition. Corneille n'a jamais pu
faire des criminels, et des pécheurs (ses plus grands criminels et ses
plus grands pécheurs), qui ne fussent éclairés de quelque reflet de
quelque lueur de la grâce, qui ne fussent nourris de quelque infiltra-
tion de la grâce, abreuvés; qui ne se sauvassent en quelque point, en
quelque sorte. De quelque manière. Et même les sacrés de Racine sont
pétris de disgrâce." (Charles Péguy, *Oeuvres Complètes* [15 vols.;
Paris: La Nouvelle Revue Française, 1916], Vol. IV, *Victor-Marie
Comte-Hugo*, 1910, p. 420.)

talent.[50] He contends that all of Racine's characters are enemies and that when they speak it is only to "mettre l'adversaire dans son tort"[51] and thus to justify, in advance, the cruelties they are going to inflict on one another, whereas Corneille's characters

> . . . au contraire, qui sont la courtoisie, la générosité même, même quand il ne veut pas, *même quand ils ne veulent pas*, ne parlent jamais que pour mettre l'adversaire, le partenaire, l'ennemi même *dans sa raison*, et ensuite vaincre litéralement cette raison.[52]
>
> Les cornéliens ne se blessent jamais, même et surtout quand ils se tuent; leur honneur alors est précisément de ne point se blesser, en un sens de ne point se faire de mal. Plus ils sont ennemis, plus ils se battent, moins aussi, moins donc ils se veulent du mal, moins ils se veulent de mal, moins ils se blessent et ils veulent se blesser.[53]

Giraudoux, who prefers Racine to Corneille, supports Péguy's contention that Corneille's characters are incapable of cruelty.[54]

While it cannot be denied that Médée and the Cléopâtre of *Rodogune* are motivated by inhuman and unnatural sentiments, Brasillach's declaration that Don Diègue and the elder Horace belong to this family of inhuman characters is not wholly justified. It has been indicated that the elder Horace is directed by a noble sentiment, however cruel it may appear to be.[55] The same argument that renders the elder Horace's act acceptable can also be applied to Don Diègue. Péguy's contention, on the other hand, is justifiable

---

[50] Cf. Péguy, *Oeuvres Choisies* (Paris: Grasset, n.d.), p. 322.
[51] *Victor-Marie Comte-Hugo*, p. 423.
[52] *Ibid.*
[53] *Ibid.*, p. 428.
[54] Cf. Giraudoux, *op. cit.*, p. 749.
[55] Cf. pp. 83-84, above.

in respect to *le Cid*, *Horace*, *Cinna*, and *Polyeucte*, but not to *Médée* or *Rodogune*. Herland offers a compromise between the ideas of Brasillach and Péguy:

> Il faut savoir gré à Brasillach d'avoir, après Schlumberger toutefois, signalé quelle galerie de monstres grimaçants forment presque tous ces pères et ces mères du théâtre de Corneille; mais nous croyons qu'il convient en conservant l'idée, de la renverser: ce n'est point tant de la haine que nous sentons chez le poète à l'égard de tous ces vieux, que de la pitié. . . . C'est que, dans l'éclairage du tragique cornélien, il n'y a pas de plus grand malheur pour un homme que de se sentir méprisé par les jeunes, même s'ils ne le montrent pas.[56]

Modern critics, unlike late-nineteenth-century critics who limited their discussions of Corneille to *le Cid*, *Horace*, *Cinna*, and *Polyeucte*, emphasize the importance of his comedies and later tragedies. Schlumberger, Brasillach, Mornet, Adam, and Herland devote fewer pages to *le Cid* than to most of Corneille's other plays. As a matter of fact, these critics have added nothing new to the generally accepted nineteenth-century interpretation of *le Cid*, which was primarily concerned with the question of duty versus love and the exercise of the hero's and heroine's wills to fulfill their duty. Sainte-Beuve was the earliest critic to point out the romanesque elements of *le Cid*[57] and the nineteenth century unanimously agreed that it was a romanesque play. The morality of the play, which so interested seventeenth- and eighteenth-century critics, was only briefly discussed during the nineteenth century. Schlumberger is the only modern critic who has felt it necessary to defend the morality of *le Cid*, and as a matter of fact, his entire discussion of the play is a defense against the charge of immorality. Schlum-

[56] *Op. cit.*, p. 93.
[57] Cf. p. 58, n. 28, above.

berger's reasons for declaring it moral are the same as those presented by his immediate predecessors.[58]

Mornet, while indicating the romanesque elements of the play, interprets *le Cid* primarily as the struggle between duty and love:

> Corneille a compris que la véritable tragédie devait se passer dans l'âme des personnages; l'émotion tragique naît de la lutte qui se livre chez Rodrigue et Chimène entre leur amour et leur devoir; le drame se transporte des événements dans la conscience, et c'est le choix de la conscience non le hasard ou la contrainte qui décident des événements et du dénouement: . . . Entre la passion et le devoir Rodrigue et Chimène choisissent sans hésiter le devoir. C'est le caractère de tous les héros cornéliens. Ou plutôt ils veulent n'agir que selon leur volonté . . . La tragédie ne mettra pas en scène des volontés aveugles, mais des volontés réfléchies.[59]

Mornet's interpretation of *le Cid* presents no new ideas.

Brasillach briefly discusses the theme of will in *le Cid* and concludes, as did the late nineteenth century, that love and not duty triumphs.[60] Following the trend of his work that emphasizes the romanesque elements of the Cornelian theater, Brasillach contends that *le Cid* is essentially a romanesque play and is the focal point of Corneille's genius:

> *Le Cid* est le centre même du génie de Corneille. . . . On comprend que cette oeuvre unique dans notre langue ait toujours conservé sa faveur. Jamais Corneille ne retrouvera cette grâce, cette jeunesse. Il y a résumé toute son expérience passée, et elle clôt un cycle. Il y a peut-être résumé ses déceptions amoureuses personnelles, en tout cas des rêves d'adolescent, le mythe qui lui est si cher de deux enfants séparés par les vieillards, ses lectures,

---

[58] Cf. *op. cit.*, pp. 56-70.
[59] *Op. cit.*, pp. 72-73.
[60] Cf. *op. cit.*, pp. 110-111.

ses ambitions romanesques et aussi le système dramatique pour lequel il était fait. . . .[61]

Adam, like Brasillach, emphasizes the romanesque elements of *le Cid*,[62] but also continues the nineteenth-century tradition that classified the play as "un drame de la volonté":

> Des hommes capables de vouloir, Rodrigue et Chimène ne sont pas emportés dans un tourbillon d'aventures comme l'avait été Clitandre, comme l'était Cléarque dans *le Prince Déguisé*. La situation où ils se débattent est romanesque. Mais c'est leur volonté qui les mène. Rodrigue décide de se battre avec le père de sa fiancée, Chimène décide de poursuivre la mort de celui qu'elle continue d'aimer. La tragi-comédie du *Cid* devenait un drame de la volonté.[63]

Herland very briefly discusses the romanesque elements of *le Cid* because, contrary to the ideas of most of his contemporaries, he does not believe that Corneille's plays basically represent the literary themes of the seventeenth century. Although Herland generally maintains that the Cornelian theater depicts the tragedy of old age, despair, and failure, he concedes that *le Cid* is characterized by a certain juvenile confidence in life that was the primary reason for its success.[64] He nonetheless declares that *le Cid* is a perfect example of what he calls "la fatalité cornélienne"; man confronted with a duty over which he has no control.[65] It cannot be denied that in this respect, Herland's interpretation of the Cornelian system is applicable to *le Cid*, but the dénouement of the play contradicts a principal element of Herland's thesis. He contends that the Cornelian theater

---

[61] *Ibid.*
[62] Cf. Adam, *op. cit.*, I, 511.
[63] *Ibid.*, p. 510.
[64] Cf. *op. cit.*, pp. 88-89.
[65] Cf. *ibid.*, p. 98.

represents "la volonté impuissante ou déchirée" because

> . . . quel autre tragique peut-on attendre d'un théâtre de l'héro-
> ïsme que celui de la déchéance du héros, ou de l'inégalité du sort
> qui interdit à jamais à tant d'hommes d'être des héros? Le
> tragique même de l'amour se ramène toujours chez Corneille à
> cette insurmontable inégalité des âmes: . . . et l'on souffre ou du
> mépris qu'on éprouve pour l'être aimé ou du mépris qu'on lui
> inspire.[66]

Late-nineteenth- and twentieth-century critics have unanimously agreed that le Cid illustrates the triumph of love
over a social convention and that everything in the play con-
spires to help liberate Rodrigue and Chimène from the fulfillment of their duty.[67] Thus Herland's thesis is not tenable
when applied to le Cid; but in all fairness to him, it should
be noted that because of the dénouement of the play, le Cid
was considered by most nineteenth-century critics an accident or exception in the Cornelian theater.[68]

Horace has always been designated the poem of patriotism and most nineteenth-century critics depicted the
younger Horace as the soldier who neither questions his
orders nor regrets his actions. The elder Horace represented a father torn between love for his country and love
for his children. Camille was considered the least typical of
Cornelian heroines because she was motivated primarily by
her love for Curiace.[69] Dorchain's[70] and Mornet's[71] inter-

---

[66] Ibid., p. 94.

[67] Cf. pp. 75-76, above.

[68] Cf. ibid.

[69] Cf. ibid., p. 78.

[70] ". . . ces deux âmes excessives . . . l'une possédée uniquement par
le patriotisme et l'autre uniquement par l'amour. . . ." (Op. cit.,
p. 202.)

[71] "Du héros impassible et traditionnel qu'est le jeune Horace,
Corneille est allé jusqu'au héros qui touche le mieux l'humanité

pretation of the younger Horace and Camille, which support the nineteenth-century attitude, is reinforced by Adam:

> Le père, tout plein du sens de l'honneur et du devoir, et qui ne distingue pas ce qu'il doit à son nom et ce qu'il doit à l'Etat, ferme, presque dur, mais humain et qui dissimule avec peine sa douleur de père. Le fils, nourri dans les idées nouvelles, totalement voué à l'Etat et à sa grandeur, fermé à tout autre sentiment, poussant jusqu'au crime son amour de la patrie. La fille, très semblable au fond à son frère, passionnée comme lui, et comme lui incapable de se partager. Toute à son amour comme il est tout à Rome.[72]

While the younger Horace has never been considered a very sympathetic character, the elder Horace, as Adam points out, is usually depicted torn between two opposing and equally strong sentiments. Brasillach, on the other hand, maintains that neither of the two Horaces receives our sympathy[73] and that the only appealing character in the play is Curiace. As a matter of fact, Brasillach's discussion of the play is almost entirely devoted to Curiace, whom he compares to the modern soldier—the conscript—rather than to the volunteer:

> Curiace est le combattant qui ne croit pas aux motifs de la gloire du droit, et qui fait son devoir de soldat, et qui meurt, sans qu'il ait réussi à faire naître en lui le partisan. . . . Tiré au sort, il est placé non pas dans la situation du jeune noble, combattant volon-

---

d'aujourd'hui (Curiace, le vieil Horace). Camille, enfin, est vivante par cette frénésie d'amour qu'on ne retrouvera plus chez aucune héroïne cornélienne. Pour aimer, elle n'a besoin ni de patrie, ni de gloire, ni même d'estime. Sa patrie c'est où vivra Curiace, sa gloire c'est de garder Curiace. . . ." (*Op. cit.*, p. 49.)

[72] *Op. cit.*, I, 525.

[73] "Ni le vieil Horace ni le jeune Horace ne touchent notre esprit et notre coeur. . . ." (*Op. cit.*, p. 138.)

taire des armées de l'ancien régime, mais dans la situation du soldat forcé des régimes démocratiques et du service militaire obligatoire. Il lui reste sa dignité, il lui reste sa protestation intérieure. . . . il est le Soldat Inconnu qui veut mourir sans être dupe.[74]

Brasillach's interpretation is tenable, but Curiace is not a principal character of the play.[75]

The major nineteenth-century criticism of *Horace* was that it violated the unity of action and that Act V was dull and useless. Although Mornet agrees that, as Faguet suggests,[76] the unity of the play is not violated if one substitutes unity of interest for unity of action, he nonetheless considers the unity of action the fundamental weakness of the play.[77] Schlumberger, on the other hand, defends the unity of action by declaring that the principal question of the play is how much one owes one's country and that this problem is not resolved until the end of Act V, when we know what will happen to the younger Horace.[78] He also declares that *Horace* does not lack unity, because the beauty of its details is intimately connected with and subordinate to the general impression of the play.[79] Although Adam, like Mornet, questions the unity of the play,[80] he reinforces Brasillach's contention that the beauty of the details is subordinate to the beauty of the whole:

---

[74] *Ibid.*

[75] Cf. p. 78, above.

[76] Cf. *ibid.*, p. 82.

[77] Cf. *op. cit.*, pp. 46-47.

[78] Cf. *op. cit.*, p. 74.

[79] Cf. *ibid.*, p. 72.

[80] "Il subsiste pourtant dans *Horace* quelques imperfections. Corneille a lui-même reconnu qu'il avait manqué à la règle de l'unité d'action en exposant son héros à deux périls successifs. . . ." (Adam, *op. cit.*, I, 523.)

. . . ce qui mérite notre admiration, ce n'est pas qu'elle observe la règle des trois unités, c'est qu'elle aboutisse à cette concentration, c'est qu'elle atteigne à cette densité sans lesquelles il n'existe pas de grande oeuvre dramatique. C'est que chaque élément du drame soit comme imbriqué dans l'ensemble, relié aux autres par des attaches nombreuses, étroites, solides, c'est que . . . les beautés de détail soient subordonnées à la beauté de l'ensemble, n'existent qu'en elle et pour elle. L'oeuvre dramatique devient ainsi un tout organique.[81]

While twentieth-century interpretations of *le Cid* and *Horace* fundamentally reinforce the ideas of late-nineteenth-century critics, there is some lack of unanimity in regard to *Cinna*. In the second half of the nineteenth century Auguste was regarded as the principal character and it was thought that this role depicted the evolution of a character.[82] Although critics contended that the unity of action was perfect, they criticized *Cinna* because there was a shift of interest from Cinna to Auguste. They also declared that Emilie was cold and inhuman and that Cinna was a rather base and cowardly character.[83]

Although Dorchain does not criticize the shift of interest in *Cinna*, he, like his predecessors, maintains that "Auguste est le véritable héros de la tragédie."[84] While he does not consider Cinna a vile and cowardly character, he admits that Cinna lacks sincerity.[85] The contention that Auguste is the principal character of the play is also supported by LeSenne, who declares that Auguste is the personification of "la vertu du pardon," which is really "la principale

---

[81] *Ibid.*, p. 524.

[82] Cf. p. 83, above.

[83] Cf. *ibid.*

[84] *Op. cit.*, p. 211.

[85] "Cinna . . . conspirateur par amour au point d'honneur de galanterie, plutôt que par conviction profonde." (*Ibid.*, p. 210.)

héroïne de la tragédie."[86] Schlumberger also reinforces the
nineteenth-century interpretation[87] and, like his predecessors,
considers Emilie's and Cinna's sincerity suspect.[88]

Brasillach, on the other hand, says that there is no shift
of interest, that Auguste is not the principal character, and
that Cinna is not base and cowardly. As a matter of fact,
he contends that Cinna is the principal hero and that the
play can be understood only if we realize that *Cinna* represents a common theme of Corneille's era, *l'amour chevaleresque* :

> ... pareil à un personnage de *l'Astrée*, Cinna est placé entre son
> serment de chevalerie amoureuse et son serment de fidélité poli-
> tique; il sacrifie tout à celle qu'il aime, et il s'avance à travers les
> trahisons et les complots comme Céladon à travers les épreuves.
> Tout n'est pour lui qu'épreuve de son amour parfait, et Cinna ne
> risquerait de nous plaire à la scène que si nous comprenions qu'il
> est vraiment le personnage principal, joli garçon élevé chez les
> Jésuites, transposant leurs leçons de domination de soi, et que si
> un metteur en scène lui restituait la barbiche à la royale et le
> grand chapeau à plumes auxquels ce faux Romain de style Louis
> XIII a droit, incontestablement.[89]

Adam's analysis of the role of Auguste as the evolution
of a character is the same as that of late nineteenth-century
critics,[90] but in all other respects he supports Brasillach's
interpretation. Adam defends Emilie against the charge of
heartlessness and Cinna against the charge of cowardice by
asserting (as does Brasillach) that these two roles repre-

---

[86] LeSenne, *Conférences de l'Odéon* (Paris: Hachette, 1916),
p. 6. LeSenne, a fervent admirer of Corneille, was instrumental in
raising funds for the statue of Corneille at the Place du Panthéon.

[87] Cf. *op. cit.*, p. 76.

[88] Cf. *ibid.*, p. 79.

[89] *Op. cit.*, p. 141.

[90] Cf. Adam, *op. cit.*, pp. 230-231.

sent the seventeenth-century ideal of *l'amour chevaleresque.* Emilie, he says, is not cold and cruel and she loves Cinna in the same manner that Chimène loves Rodrigue. Just as Chimène would not love a cowardly Rodrigue, Emilie would not love Cinna if he did not fulfill the oath he had made to her.[91] Adam's defense of Cinna is very similar to Brasillach's:

> Cinna n'est ni lâche, ni inconsistant, et l'on ne peut lui en vouloir d'être dominé par la personnalité d'Emilie . . . On dit qu'il ne sait ce qu'il veut. La vérité, c'est qu'il n'hésite pas à faire ce que l'honneur exige, mais s'aperçoit que des devoirs contraires s'imposent à lui. Ce n'est pas lâcheté, ce n'est pas inconsistance. Cinna, généreux, voit avec horreur que ses belles phrases sur la liberté dissimulaient un projet de trahison et de meurtre vulgaire. Mais il est pris par son serment, et ce mot, au XVIIe siècle, à une époque où l'esprit féodal est encore très vivant, ce mot continue de signifier quelque chose de sacré. Pris aussi par son amour pour Emilie. Un amour qui n'est point lâche, ni honteux, et qui se présente à lui avec tous les prestiges de la plus pure vertu. Cinna se sent donc déchiré. On ne peut dire pourtant qu'il hésite. Si la décision dépendait de lui, elle serait prise sans plus tarder, et Cinna renoncerait à un projet qui lui fait horreur. Mais elle dépend d'Emilie, parce qu'il l'aime, et plus encore parce qu'il a déposé son serment entre ses mains, et qu'elle seule peut l'en relever.[92]

Adam's and Brasillach's endeavor to absolve Cinna of the charge of cowardice is not completely tenable. They would have us believe that Cinna is torn between two conflicting duties over which he has no control and for which he is not responsible. Such is the situation of the elder Horace, who is confronted with duty to his country and duty to his family. Cinna's pledge to Emilie is a conscious and deliberate

[91] Cf. *ibid.,* p. 532.
[92] *Ibid.,* pp. 532-533.

decision, and the moment he makes this decision, he re-
pudiates his oath of political fidelity to Auguste, which, according to *l'honneur féodal*, is a dishonorable act. Adam's
and Brasillach's attempt to rehabilitate Cinna is interesting,
but questionable.

It will be recalled that Sainte-Beuve considered Polyeucte's martyrdom and the effect of divine grace the principal theme of *Polyeucte*.[93] Most critics in the second half
of the nineteenth century supported Sainte-Beuve's proposition, but devoted more pages to Pauline's conflict between
her love for Sévère and her love for Polyeucte.[94] Twentieth-
century critics, on the other hand, stress the religious theme.
Péguy's discussion of *Polyeucte* is concerned exclusively
with its religious implications; he considers it the most beautiful play ever written.[95] He says that both temporal and
spiritual grace are the two major elements of the Cornelian theater and that *Polyeucte*, which is based on the
effect of divine grace,[96] is the culmination of Corneille's
genius and the logical result of his first three tragedies. He
declares that the ideals of heroism and renunciation found
in *le Cid*, *Horace*, and *Cinna* are placed on the highest level
in *Polyeucte*: the spiritual level.[97] He declares that from
beginning to end of the play we are constantly aware of the
role of grace and that the play is essentially Polyeucte's
prayer to God to help all those concerned to attain the

---

[93] Cf. p. 62.

[94] Cf. pp. 88-90.

[95] Cf. *Oeuvres Complètes*, Vol. IX, *Note Conjointe sur M.
Descartes*, pp. 107-108.

[96] Cf. *ibid.*, p. 111.

[97] "*Polyeucte* n'est point une quatrième oeuvre qui vient après trois
autres . . . Les trois premières sont entre elles et sur le même plan,
elles sont trois bases et toutes les trois ensemble et au même titre elles
culminent en *Polyeucte*." (*Victor-Marie Comte-Hugo*, p. 322.)

same spiritual elevation that he experienced while being baptized:

> Tous les vers de l'intercession que nous avons marqués, que nous avons retenus dans *Polyeucte*, qui annoncent, qui introduisent, qui représentent, qui manifestent, qui déclarent, qui proclament publiquement, qui définissent pour ainsi dire techniquement l'intervention, l'intercession des saints: intercession générale des saints pour les pécheurs; applications pour ainsi dire, intercessions particulières de Néarque pour Polyeucte et de Polyeucte pour Félix et de Néarque et Polyeucte ensemble pour Pauline et les autres s'il y en a ne font qu'introduire, que présenter, quand même ils sont après, cette grande prière de Polyeucte pour Pauline en présence de Pauline qui est déjà proprement une prière d'intercession.[98]

Schlumberger devotes only a few paragraphs to the religious theme and, contrary to Péguy, declares that Corneille is incapable of creating a truly Christian atmosphere:

> Corneille, comme tout son siècle, ne sait guère mettre en valeur ce qu'on peut appeler les vertus faibles: bonté, patience, pudeur. De là vient qu'il ne peut créer une atmosphère chrétienne. . . .[99]

Both Thibaudet[100] and Mornet[101] subscribe to Péguy's interpretation, although Mornet, following the tradition of the late nineteenth century, devotes most of his discussion to Pauline's conflict. Mornet says, as do Brunetière, Lemaître, Faguet, Rigal, and Lanson, that Pauline does not love Polyeucte at the beginning of the play, but does love him at the end. In his chapter entitled "L'Ascension de

---

[98] *Ibid.*, p. 312.

[99] J. Schlumberger, "Corneille," *La Nouvelle Revue Française*, CLXXXXIII (1929), 343.

[100] Cf. A. Thibaudet, "Corneille," *La Nouvelle Revue Française*, CLXXXXIV (1929), 694.

[101] Cf. *op. cit.*, pp. 58-60.

l'Amour," Mornet supports Lanson's proposition[102] that her love for Polyeucte at the end of the play is based upon both reason and sentiment.[103]

While Péguy is primarily concerned with *Polyeucte*'s religious implications and Mornet with Pauline's dilemma between her love for Sévère and her love for Polyeucte, Brasillach considers both of these themes equally important and says that one finds in *Polyeucte* "toute le christianisme" as well as "le drame de l'amour conjugal."[104] He strongly supports Péguy's interpretation:

> *Polyeucte* est catholique non seulement par la théorie de la grâce, mais encore par la théorie des intercesseurs.[105]

He also agrees with Mornet that Pauline's love for Polyeucte is based upon reason and *estime* and, following the major theme of his work, contends that her love reflects the ideals of *l'amour courtois*:

> Déjà les spectateurs de 1640 étaient introduits au coeur du mystère par l'intermédiaire de l'amour courtois, selon la tradition de la Table Ronde et du Roman de la Rose. . . .[106]
>
> Aussi, est-ce par la porte de l'amour courtois que nous pénétrons dans le drame sacré le plus parfaitement catholique de notre temps, je veux dire *Polyeucte*.[107]

Adam briefly discusses the theme of conjugal love in *Polyeucte* and says that the couple Pauline-Sévère is more interesting than Pauline-Polyeucte.[108] He maintains that Pauline's conversion at the end cannot be explained as the

---

[102] Cf. p. 93, above.
[103] Cf. Mornet, *op. cit.*, p. 61.
[104] *Op. cit.*, p. 172.
[105] *Ibid.*, p. 174.
[106] *Ibid.*, p. 168.
[107] *Ibid.*, p. 163.
[108] Cf. *op. cit.*, I, 541.

effect of divine grace,[109] but is the result of her love for Polyeucte, which is based, as Mornet suggests, upon reason and *estime*:

> Elle veut partager les croyances de son mari, se rapprocher de lui, revivre avec lui par la communauté de la foi.[110]

Adam's interpretation emphasizes *Polyeucte*'s religious implications and reinforces Péguy's proposition that there is a constant progression from *Horace* to *Polyeucte*[111] and that the effect of divine grace is the principal element of the play:

> *Polyeucte* est la tragédie de la grâce. . . . Ce qui fait de *Polyeucte* un magnifique drame religieux, c'est que Corneille a su présenter la foi chrétienne, non comme une orthodoxie, non comme un légalisme, mais comme une vie. Dieu n'est ni l'auteur de préceptes et de formules. Il est amour, et objet d'amour. Il est une vie qui s'offre à l'âme, la pénètre, la transforme, l'élève à des hauteurs inconnues. . . . Mieux qu'une femme, mieux que la patrie, mieux que l'humanité, Dieu offre à l'homme généreux des raisons de servir, de se donner, de se dépasser. Le surnaturel ne condamne pas les vertus naturelles d'un Rodrigue ou d'un Horace. Il les couronne et les transpose sur un plan supérieur.[112]

Although it would appear that Adam supports Péguy's interpretation, he nonetheless severely criticizes the play: the motivating element in *Polyeucte*, *la grâce*, is in the realm of the supernatural and cannot be explained logically. He says that there is no action in Cornelian tragedy that cannot be explained with very precise reasons and that we know exactly what motives determine the actions of Horace,

---

[109] "Il faut quelque bonne volonté pour admettre que le Saint-Esprit soit pour quelque chose dans sa conversion." (*Ibid.*, p. 539.)

[110] *Ibid.*

[111] *Ibid.*, p. 536.

[112] *Ibid.*, pp. 537-538.

Emilie, and Auguste. He insists that the central act of the play is Polyeucte's decision to destroy the idols and that "c'est la grâce du baptême qui inspire Polyeucte."[113] This, he declares, is the weakness of the play because—

> On dira que Corneille avait déjà donné plusieurs exemples de ces revirements soudains. Mais il s'agit ici de tout autre chose. Lorsqu'Auguste ou Emilie prennent une résolution inattendue, c'est qu'ils viennent de voir avec une évidence décisive où se trouve la vérité qu'ils cherchaient depuis longtemps. Leur acte est soudain. Mais il est préparé, ne fût-ce que par cette évidence qui s'offre à eux. On cherche en vain l'évidence qui a décidé Polyeucte à un geste héroïque et insensé dans l'instant même où il venait de rassurer sa jeune femme.[114]

I believe that Adam's criticism is not tenable; as a matter of fact, his censure of *Polyeucte* is really a defense of Corneille's use of grace as the primary element of the play. Adam declares that Auguste's and Emilie's sudden decisions are the result of their having seen decisive evidence of the truth they have been looking for. Polyeucte learns about Christianity from Néarque, and if he wants to be baptized, it is presumably because he is seeking something, a true God and ways to serve him. While being baptized Polyeucte discovers, in his own manner, the truth he has been searching for and the means to serve his God.[115] Polyeucte's action is no more astonishing than Emilie's or Auguste's. The principal difference between Polyeucte's and Auguste's decisions is that Auguste's revelation serves as the denouement of the play, while Polyeucte's is the *point de départ*.

---

[113] *Ibid.*

[114] *Ibid.*

[115] Nadal defends the use of grace in *Polyeucte* in a similar manner: "c'est avec désir et besoin qu'il se tournera vers Dieu." (*Op. cit.*, p. 208.)

Conclusion

In the first half of the seventeenth century Cornelian tragedy was inevitably judged against the background of the classical doctrine that was being formulated at the time Corneille wrote his most celebrated tragedies. The three most important elements of the doctrine were that a play should be useful and pleasing; that it should be moral and have a moral aim; that it should follow the rules governing the technique of theater. The purpose of these precepts was to render a play plausible; verisimilitude was therefore a principal aim of the doctrine. In the seventeenth century verisimilitude, with its subtle overtones of *bon goût* and *bienséance*, was the ideal form that reality assumed in the mind of the public. It was in the name of verisimilitude that all the literary battles started; it was the basis of all attacks on Cornelian tragedy. Corneille's plays were often criticized on the ground that they were immoral, according to convention, and therefore incredible.

Le Cid was severely criticized by Scudéry, Mairet, d'Aubignac, and Chapelain for violating almost all the rules of the classical doctrine. These critics also declared that *le Cid* illustrated the triumph of love over duty and that Chimène's willingness to marry her father's murderer was immoral and thus incredible; *Horace*, on the other hand, evidenced Corneille's endeavor to follow the rules of accepted doctrine. The critics generally agreed that, unlike *le Cid*, *Horace* not only did not violate the rules of verisimilitude and *bienséance*, but carefully observed the unities of time and place. Their only reproach was that Camille's murder weakened the unity of action, and they condemned Act V as being unnecessary to the play. *Cinna* was generally well received by the critics, who declared that it followed the precepts of dramatic doctrine even more closely than did *Horace*: moreover, *Cinna* was not censured for failing to observe the code of verisimilitude and *bienséance*. It can be assumed that the seventeenth century saw in the role of Cinna the typical hero of the *précieux* novels of the era, who, in order to win his beloved, had to prove his merit by overcoming almost overwhelming opponents. According to Balzac, Cinna was regarded as the *honnête homme* of the play.

Although *Polyeucte* closely followed the rules of classical doctrine, it was severely criticized by most critics because religious subjects were considered inappropriate for the theater. *Polyeucte* nonetheless appealed to the spectators and critics who regarded Pauline's conflict between her love for Sévère and her duty towards Polyeucte the most important feature of the play. Mme la Dauphine's opinion that Pauline did not love her husband, but remained faithful to him out of her sense of conjugal duty, resumed the attitude of the period. Evidently at a time when marriages were arranged by parents for social and financial reasons, Pauline's conflict seemed more natural than Polyeucte's eagerness to become a martyr.

In summary it may be said that according to the critics, Corneille's greatest fault was that many of his plays did not seem plausible and often violated social as well as literary rules. Seventeenth-century critics, however, recognized in Corneille's plays an originality and a grandeur of sentiment that were lacking in the theater before his time. The term most often used in discussing Cornelian tragedy was *admiration*; critics maintained that its principal aim was to evoke admiration for the hero. Corneille's preoccupation with the grandiose and heroic, as a means of capturing the spectator's admiration, did not seem unusual, primarily because he dramatized current literary themes. The critics did not suggest that Cornelian tragedy was a conflict between duty and passion.

In the second half of the seventeenth century Corneille was criticized because he did not conform to the rule of the unities, and because his treatment of love was no longer in harmony with the temper of the time. Racinian tragedy seemed more natural and realistic. Boileau and La Bruyère nonetheless continued to declare that the characteristic feature of Cornelian tragedy was that it stimulated admiration.

Eighteenth-century critics as a rule judged Corneille's theater by the precepts of the seventeenth century. Voltaire's and La Harpe's aversion to Corneille, and their preference for Racine, were founded on sentiment of the second half of the seventeenth century. Since the dramatists of Voltaire's era accepted the classical tenets in matters of technique, it was inevitable that they too should find Cornelian tragedy defective. Their concern with analyses of love was also more in accord with the temper of their immediate predecessors than with Corneille's preoccupation with the heroic and grandiose. Voltaire and La Harpe, agreeing that Corneille's major aim was to arouse admiration, considered it a very weak principle upon which to base a tragedy.

Although Voltaire and La Harpe accepted most of the tenets of the classical doctrine as to the technique of theater, their ideas on *bon goût* and *bienséance* were not the same as those of the seventeenth century. They defended *le Cid* against the charge that the play was not plausible and that it offended *bon goût* because Chimène consented to marry Rodrigue. They found *le Cid* appealing because they considered love the most human and touching sentiment. From

Voltaire's time to the present, le Cid has not been considered immoral.

Whereas Voltaire and La Harpe reinforced seventeenth-century criticisms of Horace, their evaluation of the role of Cinna offered a marked contrast to earlier interpretations. Maintaining that Cinna was a base and cowardly character, and no longer influenced by the précieux novels, Voltaire and La Harpe were unable to understand the reasons for Cinna's actions. Most likely as a result of eighteenth-century ideas, they considered the evolution of Auguste from a tyrant to a ruler capable of forgiving his enemies the outstanding feature of the play.

Voltaire and La Harpe supported seventeenth-century criticisms of Polyeucte, but not for the same reasons. Voltaire's Zaire portrayed divine and human love, but it also illustrated the disastrous consequences of religious fanaticism; Polyeucte, on the other hand, showed the beneficial effects of divine grace and for this reason Voltaire and La Harpe disapproved of Corneille's treatment of the religious theme.

The best to be said of eighteenth-century criticisms of Corneille is that a new look at the roles of Rodrigue, Chimène, Cinna, and Auguste established a link between seventeenth- and nineteenth-century criticism.

The beginning of the nineteenth century witnessed the creation of a form of drama essentially incompatible with the classical concept of tragedy and in particular with Cornelian tragedy. Hugo, Lamartine, and Stendhal, the most fervent advocates of le drame romantique, declared that drama should depict reality. Hugo disapproved of seventeenth-century preoccupation with le beau, the transformation of reality in order to express a current ideal, and the elimination of the ugly and grotesque from all art forms. Hugo, Lamartine, and Stendhal discussed Cornelian tragedy primarily as it demonstrated, or not, the relative superiority of classical or of romantic drama. They joined in Voltaire's and La Harpe's contention that admiration is a sterile sentiment.

Janin, Nisard, and Saint-Marc Girardin asserted that Corneille's characters were not abstract or inhuman. Nisard declared that most of Corneille's plays portrayed man's conflict between duty and passion and he conveyed the impression that this conflict was the very essence of Cornelian tragedy. The terms most often used by Janin, Nisard, and Saint-Marc Girardin were the dominance of will over one's feelings, and the conflict between duty and passion.

Janin's, Nisard's, Saint-Marc Girardin's, and Sainte-Beuve's interpretation of *le Cid* supported those of Voltaire's and La Harpe's; too, they did not consider the play immoral in terms of social ethics. They generally agreed with seventeenth- and eighteenth-century criticisms of *Horace* that Camille's murder violated the unity of action. Saint-Marc Girardin regarded the elder Horace as the principal character of the play and thus continued a theme first proposed by La Harpe. This theme was to be adopted by Faguet, who offered a fresh interpretation of the play. These critics also subscribed to Voltaire's and La Harpe's criticism of *Cinna*, maintaining that Cinna was a base and cowardly character and, like their immediate predecessors, considering Auguste the principal role.

Sainte-Beuve's interpretation of *Polyeucte* was an almost complete reversal of earlier attitudes. Whereas the seventeenth and eighteenth centuries generally condemned *Polyeucte* for its religious theme, this, for Sainte-Beuve, was the play's most important feature. His interest in religion and history may have led him to interpret *Polyeucte* as a tableau of the early rise of Christianity and of the effect of divine grace. His analysis of *Polyeucte*'s religious theme was to be maintained to the present with no significant innovations. Sainte-Beuve and Saint-Marc Girardin also disagreed with their predecessors' view that Pauline was an honest and virtuous woman who didn't love her husband and that she loved Polyeucte at the end of the play. Their analysis of Pauline was also to be reaffirmed to the present.

In the second half of the nineteenth century Brunetière, Faguet, Lemaître, and Lanson re-evaluated Cornelian tragedy. Unlike their immediate predecessors, they sought out the principal elements of his theater independent of external circumstances. They modified earlier nineteenth-century implications that Cornelian tragedy depicted conflict between duty and passion. Although they agreed that *le Cid* represented such conflict, their analyses of *Horace*, *Cinna*, and *Polyeucte* clearly indicated that they did not consider it the outstanding feature of Cornelian tragedy. They did, however, support the earlier contention that one of the major aims of Corneille's theater was the glorification of man's will. Brunetière, Faguet, Lemaître, and Lanson said that the Cornelian hero believed he was free to choose his course of action and was thus the master of his destiny. They declared, particularly Lanson, that the Cornelian hero was not usually moved by sentiment. They said that the portrayal of limitless will, directed by reason, was Corneille's main aim. Although Faguet agreed that this was the outstanding feature of Corneille's theater, he maintained that it was not the aim, but the result, of Corneille's primary object: the desire to stimulate admiration. In this respect Faguet established a link between seventeenth- and late nineteenth-century attitudes. Late-nineteenth-century critics, unlike Voltaire, La Harpe, and the romantic dramatists, supported seventeenth-century attitudes by approving of Corneille's use of admiration.

As has been pointed out, the first half of the seventeenth

century did not consider Corneille's preoccupation with the grandiose and heroic unusual. Although critics in the second half of that century and throughout the eighteenth found Racinian tragedy more appealing because of its concern with human passions, they did not think that Corneille's preoccupation with more "noble" sentiments was unnatural. The nineteenth-century, certainly the late-nineteenth-century, contention that the predominant, as well as the most interesting, feature of Cornelian tragedy was the portrayal of man's will directed by reason to subdue his sentiments, was a reaction against the exaggeration of human passions by the romantic dramatists.

In respect to *le Cid* and *Horace*, Brunetière, Lemaître, and Lanson supported earlier interpretations and offered no significant innovations. Faguet, on the other hand, defended *Horace* against the seventeenth-, eighteenth-, and nineteenth-century charge that Camille's murder violated the unity of action. Corneille defined the unity of action as the unity of peril and Faguet maintained that the unity of action in *Horace* was not violated if one realized that the elder Horace was the principal character. He went on to say that the peril faced by the elder Horace was the loss of his family and that therefore Act V was necessary because it was not until Act V that we learned of the fate of the younger Horace. This interpretation was not supported by other critics.

Brunetière, Faguet, Lemaître, and Lanson also reinforced Voltaire's and La Harpe's contention that Cinna was dishonest and cowardly—evidently because Cinna was motivated by love for Emilie. They also continued the theme, first proposed by La Harpe, that Auguste was the most interesting role because it showed how man can subordinate his sentiments to more worthy motives.

These critics also subscribed to Sainte-Beuve's interpretation of *Polyeucte*, which emphasized the significance of the religious theme, and supported his claim that Pauline loved Polyeucte at the end of the play. Thus they continued an interpretation that greatly modified seventeenth- and eighteenth-century views. Although nineteenth-century interpretations of *Polyeucte* offered marked contrasts to earlier ones, they nonetheless indirectly supported the seventeenth- and eighteenth-century idea that Pauline's conflict was more interesting than Polyeucte's martyrdom.

In the twentieth century the works of Dorchain, Rivaille, Schlumberger, Brasillach, Adam, Nadal, and Herland illustrate three important trends. They condemn the tendency of their immediate predecessors to systematize Cornelian tragedy as a glorification of will. Although many eighteenth- and nineteenth-century critics suggested, in passing, that Corneille's plays often depicted events that actually occurred in the dramatist's life, as well as current literary and philosophical ideas, no literary critic before the twentieth century seriously developed this aspect of Cornelian tragedy. The third trend is concern for Corneille's comedies and for those tragedies written after *Rodogune*. Nineteenth-century critics discussed at length *le Cid*, *Horace*, *Cinna*, and *Polyeucte*, and referred to the comedies and later tragedies only when they wanted to emphasize some aspect of his theater. Twentieth-century critics, on the other hand, attach more importance to the comedies and later tragedies. These three trends are intimately related. The importance assigned to Corneille's comedies and later tragedies, together with the attempt to show that his plays were influenced by contemporary literary, political, and philosophical ideas, is a reaction against the systematization of Cornelian tragedy by late-nineteenth-century critics.

Twentieth-century critics maintain that there are other elements of Corneille's theater, especially its romanesque tendencies, that are just as important as the theme of *vo-*

lonté, if not more so. As a matter of fact they have attempted to show that the use of will to overcome sentiment was a common theme of seventeenth-century *précieux* novels.

The fundamental difference between their interpretations of *le Cid* and *Horace* and those of the nineteenth century is that twentieth-century critics assert that these two plays dramatized the ideas of the period and that Corneille did not invent new themes. Brasillach's and Adam's interpretation of *Cinna* is perhaps the most striking example. In the seventeenth century Cinna was considered the *honnête homme* of the play; from Voltaire's time he was called a cowardly and dishonest character. Brasillach and Adam have established a link between seventeenth- and twentieth-century ideas by declaring that Cinna is not cowardly if we understand that he represents a common theme of Corneille's era: *l'amour chevaleresque* of a hero of *l'Astrée* torn between his oath of political fidelity and his oath of love.

Twentieth-century critics, like those of the nineteenth century, stress the importance of *Polyeucte*'s religious theme and maintain that Pauline loved Polyeucte at the end of the play. Brasillach and Adam agree with their predecessors that Pauline's love is based upon reason and sentiment, but emphasize that the evolution of her love reflects the ideals of *l'amour courtois*.

The contributions of modern critics are of major importance as regards the sources of Corneille's ideas and themes. While they do not deny that will is an important feature of Cornelian tragedy, their proposition that its predominant themes reflected contemporary social, literary, and philosophical trends departs considerably from nineteenth-century views, which seemed to imply that Corneille invented those themes. Their aim has been not to depreciate Corneille's originality, but to indicate the immense scope and complexities of his talent.

Bibliography

BOOKS CONSULTED

Adam, A. *Histoire de la Littérature Française au XVIIe Siècle.* 5 vols. Paris: Domat, 1949-1956.

Beaumarchais, P. *Théâtre Complet.* Paris: Gallimard, 1949.

Bénichou, P. *Morales du Grand Siècle.* Paris: 1940.

Boileau, N. *Oeuvres.* Paris: Garnier, 1952.

Brasillach, R. *Corneille.* Paris: Arthème Fayard, 1938.

Bray, R. *La Formation de la Doctrine Classique en France.* Paris: Nizet, 1951.

————. *La Tragédie Cornélienne devant la Critique Classique— d'après la Querelle de Sophonisbe* 1663. Paris: Hachette, 1927.

Brunetière, F. *Etudes Critiques sur l'Histoire de la Littérature Française.* Paris: Hachette, 1891.

————. *Les Epoques du Théâtre Français.* Paris: Hachette, 1896.

Caro, E. *La Fin du dix-huitième Siècle.* Paris: Hachette, 1880.

Corneille, P. *Oeuvres.* 2 vols. Paris: La Pléiade, 1950.

Dorchain, A. *Pierre Corneille.* Paris: Garnier, 1918.

Faguet, E. *En lisant Corneille.* Paris: Hachette, 1914.

————. *Propos de Théâtre.* Paris: Société Française d'Imprimerie et de Librairie, 1903-1905.

————. *Etudes Littéraires.* Vol. III. Paris: Lecène, Oudin, 1894.

Gaiffe, F. *Le Drame en France au XVIIIe Siècle.* Paris: Armand Colin, 1907.

Gasté, A. *La Querelle du Cid.* Paris: H. Welter, 1898.

Herland, L. *Corneille.* Paris: Editions du Seuil, 1954.

Hugo, V. *Cromwell.* Paris: Flammarion, 1827.

Janin, J. *Rachel et la Tragédie.* Paris: Amyot, 1859.

————. *Histoire de la Littérature Dramatique.* 6 vols. Paris: Lévy, 1854.

Joannidès, A. *La Comédie-Française de 1680 à 1920.* Paris: Plon, 1921.

La Bruyère, J. *Les Caractères.* Paris: Garnier, 1952.

La Harpe, J. *Cours de Littérature Ancienne et Moderne.* 3 vols. Paris: Firmin-Didot, 1851.

Lamartine, A. de. *Cours Familier de Littérature.* 28 vols. Paris: 1856-1869.

Lanson, G. *Corneille.* Paris: Hachette, 1898.

Lemaître, J. *Pierre Corneille.* Vol. IV of *Histoire de la Langue et de la Littérature Française.* Published under the direction of L. Petit de Julleville. Paris: Armand Colin, 1897.

———. *Impressions de Théâtre.* Paris: Boivin, 1886-1889.

LeSenne. *Conférences de l'Odéon.* Paris: Hachette, 1916.

Magne, E. *Voiture et l'Hôtel de Rambouillet.* 2 vols. Paris: Garnier, 1911.

Mornet, D. *Histoire Générale de la Littérature Française.* Paris: Larousse, n.d.

Nadal, O. *Le Sentiment de l'Amour dans l'Oeuvre de Pierre Corneille.* Paris: Gallimard, 1948.

Nisard, D. *Histoire de la Littérature Française.* 3 vols. Firmin-Didot, 1881.

Péguy, C. *Oeuvres Choisies.* Paris: Grasset, n.d.

———. *Oeuvres Complètes.* Vol. IV: *Victor-Marie Comte-Hugo.* Vol. IX: *Note Conjointe sur M. Descartes.* Paris: La Nouvelle Revue Française, 1916.

Rigal, E. *De Jodelle à Molière.* Paris: Hachette, 1911.

Rivaille, L. *Les Débuts de P. Corneille.* Paris: Boivin, 1936.

Saint-Evremond, C. de *Oeuvres.* Paris: Garnier, 1866.

———. *Letters.* Edited by J. Hayward. London: Routledge and Sons, 1930.

Saint-Marc Girardin, F. *Cours de Littérature Dramatique.* 5 vols. Paris: Charpentier, 1868.

Sainte-Beuve, C. *Port-Royal.* 2 vols. Paris: Gallimard, 1953.

———. *Nouveaux Lundis.* Paris: Lévy, 1867.

———. *Histoire de la Littérature Française.* 4 vols. Paris: La Renaissance du Livre, n.d.

Sarcey, F. *Quarante Ans de Théâtre*. Paris: Bibliothèque des Annales, 1900.

Schlumberger, J. *Plaisir à Corneille*. Paris: Gallimard, 1936.

Sévigné, Mme de. *Lettres*. 12 vols. Paris: Hachette, 1862.

Stendhal. *Racine et Shakspeare*. 2 vols. Paris: Champion, 1925.

Voltaire. *Commentaires sur Corneille*. Paris: Firmin-Didot, 1862.

———. *Le Siècle de Louis XIV*. 2 vols. Paris: Garnier, 1947.

ARTICLES CONSULTED

Giraudoux, J. "Racine," *La Nouvelle Revue Française*, Vol. CLXXXXV (1929).

Schlumberger, J. "Corneille," *La Nouvelle Revue Française*, Vol. CLXXXXIII (1929).

Thibaudet, A. "Corneille," *La Nouvelle Revue Française*, Vol. CLXXXXIV (1929).